ROUTLEDGE LIBRARY EDITIONS: SEMANTICS AND SEMIOLOGY

Volume 1

ON THE SEMANTICS OF *WH*-CLAUSES

ON THE SEMANTICS
OF *WH*-CLAUSES

STEPHEN BERMAN

Routledge
Taylor & Francis Group

LONDON AND NEW YORK

First published in 1994 by Garland Publishing, Inc.

This edition first published in 2017
by Routledge
2 Park Square, Milton Park, Abingdon, Oxon OX14 4RN

and by Routledge
711 Third Avenue, New York, NY 10017

Routledge is an imprint of the Taylor & Francis Group, an informa business

British Library Cataloguing in Publication Data
A catalogue record for this book is available from the British Library

ISBN: 978-1-138-69750-8 (Set)
ISBN: 978-1-315-52029-2 (Set) (ebk)
ISBN: 978-1-138-69076-9 (Volume 1) (hbk)
ISBN: 978-1-138-69081-3 (Volume 1) (pbk)
ISBN: 978-1-315-53671-2 (Volume 1) (ebk)

Publisher's Note
The publisher has gone to great lengths to ensure the quality of this reprint but
points out that some imperfections in the original copies may be apparent.

Disclaimer
The publisher has made every effort to trace copyright holders and would welcome
correspondence from those they have been unable to trace.

ON THE SEMANTICS OF *WH*-CLAUSES

STEPHEN BERMAN

GARLAND PUBLISHING, Inc.
New York & London / 1994

Library of Congress Cataloging-in-Publication Data

Berman, Stephen, 1961–
     On the semantics of Wh-clauses / Stephen Berman.
         p.   cm. — (Outstanding dissertations in linguistics)
     Includes bibliographical references and index.
     ISBN 0–8153–1742–5 (alk. paper)
     1. Grammar, Comparative and general—Syntax.   2. Semantics.
3. Generative grammar.   I. Title.   II. Series.
P295.B47   1994
415—dc20   93–46330
                                                                                    CIP

Printed on acid-free, 250-year-life paper
Manufactured in the United States of America

Contents

Preface

This book contains the essentially unaltered text of my doctoral dissertation in linguistics, submitted to the Graduate School of the University of Massachusetts, Amherst, in January 1991. I have shortened the title (from *On the Semantics and Logical Form of* Wh-*Clauses*), both to make it less cumbersome and to place greater emphasis on the fact that an investigation and analysis of the interpretation of *wh*-clauses constitutes the original work presented here; while Logical Form is made use of in chapter V, I do not offer new arguments for this level of representation, and, as I acknowledge there, my results could be maintained (in somewhat different form) without appealing to LF. I have also augmented the bibliography with a few references to published versions of works I originally cited in unpublished form; but I have left the original references in the text, since it is these I used in my writing. The text itself contains no substantive changes; I have merely corrected several typographical errors and changed the wording in numerous places to conform to the book format.

In the nearly three years since I finished writing the dissertation, I have pursued the development of certain aspects of it. In addition, several works have appeared that respond directly to some of the central points of the research I report on here; I refer specifically to Lahiri (1991), Groenendijk and Stokhof (1992), and Ginzburg (1992; 1993) (see the bibliography for detailed listings of these and other works cited in this preface). In the remainder of this preface I will briefly summarize both my own further research as well relevant aspects of these works and indicate what I take to be their significance for my proposals. This is not the place for a comprehensive review, nor for in depth argumentation or an explicit formal exposition; these are contained in the manuscript, which as I write is still in progress, upon which these cursory remarks are based.

Concerning the formal framework of my analysis, which I referred to as "the Lewis/Heim/Kamp theory," I have more recently implemented it directly in the formalism of Discourse Representation Theory, as codifed in Kamp and Reyle (1993). While my original "flat" representations have, as I pointed out (chapter I, note 7), the advantage of compactness, Discourse Representation Structures are rather more perspicuous. Along with this superficial change I have also adopted the current position of DRT, different from that of Lewis (1975), Kamp (1981), and Heim (1982), that quantifiers—even adverbial ones—are not inherently unselective but rather, by various means (*e.g.* focus), in a given context always quantify over specified variables. The reason for this has to do with the proportion problem, which I alluded to (chapter I, note 8) but did not attempt to deal with. To account for instances of simultaneous quantification, which constituted the impetus for unselective binding, quantifiers are allowed, however, to "select" different variables, including multiple variables, in different contexts. Such quantifiers are known as polymorphous; Chierchia (1992) provides a basic discussion of these.

Using DRSs has also facilitated elaboration of the role of presupposition within my analysis by enabling me to incorporate the presupposition theory of van der Sandt (1992), which is formulated in terms of DRT. Van der Sandt has proposed a variety of pragmatic and structural principles for accounting for the projection behavior of presuppositional material in discourse. Part of this includes the notion of presupposition accommodation, which plays a central role in my analysis. Van der Sandt argues that there is no theoretical distinction between global and local accommodation, rather there is a general preference principle to accommodate as high up in the DRS as possible, while adhering to the pragmatic and structural constraints. It is the interaction of these principles that results in the descriptive difference between global, *i.e.* top-level, accommodation and accommodation at various lower levels, which is more or less "local".

One of van der Sandt's structural principles is an injunction against creating free variables, which he uses to account for presupposition projection in quantified utterances. I have attempted to apply this analysis to the interaction between presupposition and adverbs of quantification. Consider the derivation of the logical representation (27.a), discussed on pages 53-55. Since the nuclear scope contains presuppositional material, according to van der Sandt's theory this should be accommodated as high up as possible. But this presuppositional material is an open sentence, so accommodating it to the top level will result in a structure with free variables. Accommodating it to the next level down, the restrictive term, however, results in the variables being bound by the quantifier, yielding the desired—and required—representation. This account thus seems to provide a motivated explanation for the stipulation (or rather, the observation) that the presuppositions of the nuclear scope of a quantifier become part of its restrictive term.

The account cannot, however, be complete as given. For one thing, DRT does in fact allow free variables (*i.e.*, discourse referents) at the top level, which may be existentially interpreted or assigned a contextual referent (I briefly allude to this in the discussion of definiteness in appendix B). This possibility manifests itself particularly in the contrast between generic (or habitual) and episodic sentences. I did not bring this into my analysis, though I drew attention to it in the discussion of *if*-clauses on page 45. But I have since attempted to treat it, by developing the sketchy remarks of appendix B. It seems that in episodic sentences there is what appears to be simultaneous global and local accommodation, the former providing the context set, the latter the restrictive term. However, this possibility does not appear to be directly compatible with van der Sandt's presupposition theory. An alternative, one which I am continuing to explore, is that the quantifier, as a (possibly contextually triggered) lexical property, requires, or selects, certain variables, and that the context set supplies these. This idea fits well with the treatment of quantifiers as polymorphous rather than unselective. Working it out in detail is, however, rather complicated, involving the introduction of variables (or discourse referents) over situations and other eventualities, and of the accompanying semantic apparatus (these are treated at length in Kamp and Reyle (1993, chapter 5)); I refrain from further elaboration at this juncture.

Closely connected with the preceding considerations, and also broached in appendix B, is the analysis of plurality. I have attempted to bring this into the scope of my analysis (also prompted by the discussion in Lahiri (1991)—see below), drawing largely on the treatment in Kamp and Reyle (1993). The need to distinguish plural and singular NPs arises from the quantificational behavior of definites, including *which*-phrases, alluded to at several points in the text. Their semantics requires enriching the model theory by imposing an algebraic structure on the domain of individuals (thus giving these a similar structure to that of situations). But doing so allows a considerable increase in the empirical coverage of the analysis: bringing into focus parallels and asymmetries not only between indefinites and *wh*-phrases, which my original work emphasized, but also between these phrase types and definites; and concomitantly encompassing a wider range of clause types, specifically *that*-clauses; and finally, revealing the effect of presupposition in all these constructions. Thus, the scope of the project is now much broader than the more modest aims of my dissertation; but there remains much work to do in order to flesh out the ideas hinted at here.

There are several others aspects of my original analysis that I have since either elaborated or altered; I do not have space here to touch on all of them, but some I will address in the course of discussing the works I mentioned above that respond to it, to which I now turn, starting with Lahiri (1991). This is a quite detailed critical examination of my original analysis and contains numerous suggestions, based on data I had not taken into consideration, for amending it, while staying within its basic assumptions. But on a couple of points Lahiri concludes that my approach is fundamentally flawed, and therefore proposes an alternative analysis. The "friendly" amendments concern data involving presupposition, plurality, and default quantification. His alternative is prompted by flaws he see in my account of the distribution of *wh*-clauses and by the behavior of certain multiple-*wh*-clauses. Let me briefly elaborate on these points.

Lahiri rightly notes that I neglected to analyse the role of presupposition in examples where factivity is not at issue; in fact, any presuppositions in the nuclear scope become part of the restrictive term (modulo the remarks above concerning global accommodation and context sets). Lahiri cites as examples the predicates *be certain about* and *agree on*: the first presupposes something like 'consider it likely that p', where p is the proposition (or open sentence) embedded under *be certain about*; the second presupposes something like 'believe that p'. These presuppositions (*i.e.*, the open sentences corresponding to them) serve to restrict the adverbial quantifier in a sentence like *For the most part, the women are certain about/agree on who came*. This is as expected on my analysis.

The predicate *agree on* also brings to attention the need to treat plurality, since it requires a plural subject. Lahiri shows that my original analysis fails to yield intuitively correct truth conditions for sentences involving this predicate under the assumption of a default universal quantifier. But he also shows that incorporating an adequate semantics for plurality, which as I indicated above is in any case required and does not necessitate essential changes in my basic analysis, does produce the desired results.

The criticism concerning default quantificational force is somewhat specious, since I cite Hintikka's examples of default existential force and explicitly acknowledge (*e.g.*, chapter III, note 4) that universal force is a simplifying assumption on my part. Lahiri himself does not offer a comprehensive alternative, suggesting only that it may be a contextually influenced lexical matter. Nevertheless, prompted by Lahiri's critique, I have examined a range of data and believe that the ambiguity in default quantificational force only arises in the case of *wh*-clauses with simple *wh*-words (*e.g. who*), and not with *which*-phrases (compare *John told me who he saw at the party.* with *John told me which students he saw at the party.*). I do not yet have a fully satisfying theoretical account of this, but the observation is significant, I believe, in light of the considerations that lead Lahiri to seek an alternative to my basic analysis. I return to these after discussing his criticism of my account of the distribution of *wh*-clauses.

One of the principal claims of my analysis is that the interpretation of *wh*-clauses is dichotomous, being either a question-denoting entity or an open sentence that serve as a quantifier restriction, due to presupposition accommodation (the denotation in a given context arises from the presence of a question operator or a quantifier, conditioned in embedded contexts by lexical properties of the embedding predicates). As Lahiri notes, on this account it would be expected that all factive predicates can embed a *wh*-clauses (in fact, Hintikka (1976) comes close to proposing this, in terms of his notion of 'success presupposition', which I refer to on page 23). This is not the case (*e.g. regret*), and the way I avoid this result is by appealing to subcategorization (though I do not dwell on this, but *cf.* chapter V, note 18). Lahiri points out that Pesetsky (1982) has suggested that subcategorization can be eliminated from the grammar, its job being done by the independently motivated modules of semantic selection and Case theory. But Rothstein (1992) has shown that Pesetsky's account does not succeed with a wide range of data, and concludes that some reference to subcategorization is (still) necessary. (However, Pesetsky (1993) has suggested amendments to his account that he claims counter Rothstein's objections; thus the matter is still open.)

Lahiri further observes that using both subcategorization and selection information, as I do, leads to the *prima facie* expectation of six types of clause-embedding predicate (with respect to the distribution of *wh*-clauses), while only three are realized. This prompts his alternative analysis, according to which *wh*-clauses are uniformly question-denoting entities. To account for their distribution under embedding, however, he proposes that the embedding predicates not only select the semantic type of their complement (question or proposition) but also specify with what type they may grammatically combine. This bifurcation produces the same six possible clause-embedding predicates as on my analysis. Lahiri introduces various mechanisms and stipulations to yield only the three occurring types, but upon examination I have concluded that these are no better motivated than the stipulations I have to make in terms of subcategorization. In short, I find that my account of the distribution of *wh*-clauses remains viable.

　　　Finally, let me address Lahiri's most compelling, if somewhat subtle, argument against my analysis. This concerns multiple-*wh*-clauses embedded under predicates that do not distribute over conjunctions in the embedded clause. An example is the following sentence:

(*)　　It surprised Peter that Prof. Jones spoke to Maria and Prof. García spoke to Bill.

One can construct convincing models in which this sentence is true while at the same time it is neither true that it surprised Peter that Prof. Jones spoke to Maria nor that it surprised him that Prof. García spoke to Bill. Moreover, the same models verify the corresponding sentence with a *wh*-clause:

(**)　　It surprised Peter who spoke to whom.

Lahiri's claim is that my analysis, on which quantification is over values of the *wh*-phrases, cannot render these truth conditions. He shows that an analysis on which quantification is not over an algebraically structured domain of individuals but rather over such a structured domain of propositions—namely, the propositions that result from assigning values to the *wh*-phrases, does yield the desired truth conditions. He goes on to analyse quantificational variability also in these terms.

　　　If Lahiri's claim were correct, my analysis would indeed seem to be falsified. However, in conversation Ede Zimmermann has shown that it is possible to get Lahiri's results while maintaining quantification over a domain of individuals, specifically in the case of (**) pairs of individuals. I refrain from going into the technical details in the present context, but the conclusion is that it is not necessary to go to the level of propositions; rather, one can maintain the basic form of my analysis in terms of quantification over (an appropriately structured) domain of individuals.

In connection with this argument let me note that Lahiri does not base his claim especially on sentences like (**), but maintains that the same truth conditions hold for corresponding sentences with *which*-phrases, *e.g.*, *It surprised Peter which professors spoke to which students*. It is not, however, clear to me that this is so. That is, I'm not sure that there isn't a distributive entailment in this case, in contrast to (**), though to elaborate on this would be too involved for this sketch. Let me just note that I suspect that default quantificational force plays a role here, based on my observation, referred to above, that *which*-phrase seem only to allow default universal force, while simple *wh*-words allow in addition default existential force. As of this writing, I am still pursuing this line of investigation.

This concludes my discussion of Lahiri (1991); I turn now to Groenendijk and Stokhof (1992). This article is a response to my argument against analysing *wh*-clauses as inherently exhaustive, as in Groenendijk and Stokhof (1982; 1984). First, they accept my empirical claims regarding quantificational variability. They proceed to augment their original analysis with dynamic semantics (see Groenendijk and Stokhof (1990; 1991) and Chierchia (1992) for presentations), which they claim allows them to account for this variability. Second, they nevertheless maintain that strong exhaustiveness, in the sense discussed in chapter IV, is desirable even with quantificational variability.

Regarding the first point, Irene Heim has pointed out to me in conversation that Groenendijk and Stokhof's attempt to incorporate dynamic semantics into their semantics for questions contains a formal error, having to do with the representation of quantification that is not definable in terms of the standard truthfunctional connectives of the first-order predicate calculus (see chapter I, pages 8-9). Thus, an account of quantificational variability in terms of their semantics for questions remains wanting. (Ginzburg (1993) refers to Groenendijk and Stokhof's attempt to treat quantificational variability, citing Groenendijk and Stokhof (1993), which I have not seen. This appears to be a later version of their (1992) paper but I do not know if it corrects the error in the earlier version.)

As for the case against strong exhaustiveness, I stand by my contention, detailed in chapter IV, that this is not an inherent property of *wh*-clauses. There I acknowledged that with predicates like *know* this sometimes seems to have counterintuitive consequences, which I attempted to account for by appealing to Gricean conversational principles. An alternative explanation may be possible by taking into account the results of Heim (1993). She shows that it is possible to generalize Karttunen's (1977) analysis of question-embedding predicates so as to deliver strongly exhaustive meanings, without making the question-meaning itself strongly exhaustive. This opens the possibility of treating (strong) exhaustiveness purely as a lexical property of given predicates, a strategy in principle compatible with my analysis. And bearing in mind that Karttunen's analysis is in essence a special case of Hamblin's semantics for questions, where the meaning is restricted to true answers—see the discussion in chapter II—Heim's results should be replicable in Hamblin's terms, thus directly importable into my original analysis.

I close this preface by referring briefly to Ginzburg's (1992; 1993) analysis. This is concerned primarily with providing a comprehensive account of the question/answer relation, which is orthogonal to the main points of my analysis. Nevertheless, Ginzburg's investigation leads him to make a binary division between question-embedding predicates (*i.e.*, in my terms, *wh*-clause-embedding predicates), that essentially replicates my (pragmatically conditioned) factivity-based distinction. I refrain here from going into any of the formal differences between our approaches (Ginzburg's is implemented in the framework of situation semantics), but I will comment on Ginzburg's discussion of quantificational variability.

His contention is that this is not a matter of quantifying over values of the *wh*-phrases at all but rather that the adverb modifies the degree to which the values of the *wh*-clause (*i.e.*, the answer to the question the *wh*-clause denotes) resolve the question with respect to the embedding predicate. Resolution is defined in terms of an algebra of information, with resolving items of information being factual. Ginzburg motivates his proposal with examples such as the following. He says that a situation where Celia only knows that some unruly linguists showed up last night, though she doesn't know who they are, may be truthfully reported by the sentence *Celia knows to some extent who showed up last night.* He observes that in this situation Celia is not claimed to have any knowledge of specific individuals, which is what my analysis (with *to some extent* translated as a restricted existential quantifier) entails.

I believe that what Ginzburg draws attention to is a use of many adverbial quantificational expressions that is logically independent of the individual-quantifying use I have analysed. Evidence for this is the fact that the same sentence may without contradiction or even a sense of infelicity contain adverbials with conflicting quantificational forces, as in *For the most part, Celia knows only to some extent who showed up last night.* I understand this as asserting that for most people who showed up Celia has only limited knowledge of who they are. But on Ginzburg's account, this sentence should assert that Celia's knowledge simultaneously resolved the question of who showed up both to a majority degree and to a minority degree, which appears to be contradictory. (Since Ginzburg also parametrizes resolvedness with respect to goals, he might contend that the two adverbials modify knowledge relative to distinct goals. But note that one of these "goals" is simply that of counting individuals and not, like the other goal, modifying the quality of knowledge attributed. These seem to me sufficiently different to warrent distinct treatments.) Another observation is that some adverbial expressions only seem to function as quantifiers over individuals, *e.g.*, *without exception*, which is unexpected on Ginzburg's account. In short, I take it that quantificational variability is a distinct phenomenon from the degree of question resolvedness.

This concludes my overview of developments of and reactions to my thesis since its writing. I hope to have given some indication that my principal original claims have so far stood up to scrutiny, also that my analysis is flexible enough to incorporate amendments designed to take a wider range of data into account. I also believe that the fact that my research has generated further research in the same domain shows that this remains a fruitful area of investigation in natural language semantics.

Stuttgart, November 1993

Acknowledgments

I thank the members of my doctoral committee, under whose guidance I conducted the research documented here: Edmund L. Gettier, F. Roger Higgins, Barbara H. Partee, David Pesetsky, and especially Angelika Kratzer, my committee chair, without whose interest in and attention to my research the resulting dissertation would have been much poorer. I am also grateful to all the people from whom I received feedback on this work throughout its genesis: fellow students at UMass as well as participants at various conferences and colloquia at which I presented parts of this material. And I would like particularly to thank Ede Zimmermann for many helpful discussions during the final months of writing.

On the Semantics
of *Wh*-Clauses

I

Introduction

1 Overview

This study is concerned with certain kinds of *wh*-clauses, whose interpretations are easily and, I will argue, plausibly rendered by a logicosemantic analysis on which *wh*-phrases translate as open sentences, that is, as expressions of the semantically interpreted representation which contain free variables. The evidence for my analysis is drawn almost entirely from English, though I briefly cite data suggesting the analysis carries over to Japanese as well, and the same holds for German, as I have gathered from discussions with a number of native speakers (though I do not report the evidence here); I am thus reasonably confident that the basic form of the analysis is of quite genereral relevance to the linguistic issues raised by it.

The *wh*-constructions I treat at length are what are traditionally called indirect and direct questions.[1] The evidence I will be presenting indicates that the sentences that embed indirect questions constitute a semantically inhomogeneous class, consisting of those interpreted as quantified sentences, and those interpreted in the same way as direct questions. On my analysis, (1.a) may have the same interpretation as (1.b), and the embedded clause in (1.c) may have the same interpretation as (1.d); but (1.a) and (1.c) do not have the same intepretation.

(1)   a.   The teacher always finds out which students arrive late.
      b.   If a student arrives late, the teacher always finds out.
      c.   The teacher always wonders which students arrive late.
      d.   Which students arrive late?

Following the usual line of research in logical semantics, I will use the intuitive truth conditions (which, for explicitness, will be formulated in terms of modeltheoretic semantics) of sentences such as these to argue for a particular logical analysis, and will try to relate the logical representations thus obtained to the syntactic representations of the sentences by means of general grammatical processes. On the analysis I will present, the *wh*-phrase *which students* and the indefinite noun phrase *student* have the same logical translation, namely, student'(x).[2] This means that meaning differences among the sentences in (1) will have to be accounted for in other ways. Two of the aims of my research are to justify this uniform logical analysis and to offer an account of the observed differences.

The idea that NPs such as those in (1) are logically open sentences is not new; in particular, this treatment of indefinites is a cornerstone of the closely related Discourse Representation Theory of Kamp (1981) and File Change Semantics of Heim (1982). (Kamp originally applied this idea only to indefinites, Heim to definites as well.[3]) The extension of this idea to *wh*-phrases is due to Nishigauchi (1986; 1990); he does not, however, develop an explicit semantic analysis for *wh*-phrases based on this idea, nor explore the consequences of it for the semantics of *wh*-clauses. The main goal of my investigation is to do just this; this turns out to result in a semantics for *wh*-clauses that differs sharply from the infuential line extending from Baker (1968) through Karttunen (1977) to Groenendijk and Stokhof (1982; 1984), though it bears conceptual similarities to the treatment of Hintikka (1976), for one class of these sentences, and to that of Hamblin (1973), for the other.

Since the analysis of indefinite (and definite) NPs as open sentences has been convincingly carried out by Heim and Kamp, the bulk of the original work in this study is concerned with applying this analysis to *wh*-phrases. I will thus confine myself, in the remainder of this introduction, to a summary of relevant aspects of the Kamp/Heim theory, sufficient to provide the theoretical basis for my analysis of *wh*-clauses. I will concentrate, in particular, on the form and model-theoretic interpretation of the logical translations generated in this theory, putting aside numerous significant, but for present purposes extraneous, details, such as the status of discourse referents and the dynamic aspects of the semantics, as well as the compositional constructions of the logical representations. In order to set the stage for my analysis, I devote chapter II to a brief review of some of the more influential recent analyses of the semantics of questions, concentrating on issues related to the truthconditional interpretation of these constructions. Then in chapter III I give the first part of my analysis, concentrating on logicosemantic similarities between *wh*-phrases and indefinite NPs, *i.e.*, dealing with sentences such as those in (1a-b). In chapter IV I take up some challenges to my analysis and attempt to refute them. In chapter V I extend the analysis to account for asymmetries between *wh*-phrases and indefinites, and also deal with sentences such as those in (1.c-d). In appendices I discuss several issues raised by my analysis, that are somewhat peripheral to its central points, and in need of further research.

2 The Lewis/Heim/Kamp Theory

2.1 Motivation

One of the most compelling facts suggestive of analysing indefinites as open sentences, apparently first noted in a theoretical context by Lewis (1975), is their quantificational variability, that is, their ability to display a variety of quantificational forces, depending on the sentence they are in. The sentences in (2) illustrate this ((2.a,b) are Lewis's (12) and (9), respectively):

(2) a. A quadratic equation usually has two different solutions.
     b. Riders on the Thirteenth Avenue line seldom find seats.
     c. If a farmer owns a donkey, he takes good care of it.
     d. If a graduate student submits a paper to *LI*, it is often rejected.

These sentences may be paraphrased as follows:

(3) a. Most quadratic equations have two different solutions each.
     b. For few riders on the Thirteenth Avenue line is there a seat that they each find (when they ride on the Thirteenth Avenue line).
     c. For all pairs of a farmer and a donkey such that the farmer owns the donkey, the farmer takes good care of the donkey.

> d. For many pairs of a graduate student and a paper such that
>   the graduate student submits the paper to *LI*, the paper is
>   rejected.

Classically, indefinites are analyzed as existentially quantified (*e.g.* in
Russell (1919); *cf.* Heim (1982) for discussion); for instance, the
logical representation of a sentence containing the NP *a donkey* would
always include at least the formula in (4):

(4) $\exists x[...donkey'(x)...]$

But the quantificational variability exhibited by the indefinites in the
sentences in (2) seems to be prima facie evidence against such an
analysis. But then where do the quantificational forces of the indefinites
in these sentences come from? For the first two and fourth sentences, it
seems clear that it is the adverb: (2.a) has to do with most quadratic
equations (<*usually*), (2.b) with few riders on the Thirteenth Avenue
line (<*seldom*), (2.d) with many pairs of a graduate student and a paper
s/he submits to LI (<*often*). In view of this apparent ability of these
adverbs to "give" their quantificational force to indefinites, Lewis called
them adverbs of quantification.[4]

Putting aside for a moment the source of the universal force of
the indefinites in (2.c), where there is no explicit adverb of quantification, the data in (2) suggest that, instead of their translation always
being associated with an existential quantifier, indefinites are inherently
nonquantified, so that the logical representation of a sentence containing the NP *a donkey*, for example, would, in contrast to the above,
only have to contain at least the formula in (5), with the variable free
to be bound in principal by any quantifier with scope over it, not
necessarily an existential one.

(5) $[...donkey'(x)...]$

This is the conclusion drawn by Heim (1982) from data such as the
sentences in (2), though not by Lewis himself.[5] I will occasionally
follow Heim (1983a) in calling this the nonquantificational analysis of
indefinites, though often, for brevity, I will refer to it as the LHK
theory (for Lewis/Heim/Kamp).

If we consult again the paraphrases in (3) of the sentences in (2), several other properties may be noticed. So from (3.b) we see that although the indefinite *riders on the Thirteenth Avenue line* in (2.b) does have the quantificational force of the adverb *seldom,* the indefinite *seats* does not, but instead has merely an existential reading; this raises the questions, when do indefinites get what we might call the quantificational interpretation and when are they existentially interpreted, and also, what is the source of the existential interpretation? Secondly, as (3.d) makes clear, more than one indefinite in a sentence can simultaneously receive the quantificational force of a single adverb of quantification; this observation led Lewis to treat these adverbs as unselective quantifiers, *i.e.*, quantifiers that can in principle bind any free variables in their scope. Of course, unselectivity must be constrained, since, as just noted, sometimes indefinites are not quantified by an adverb of quantification, though in its scope; so the question to be answered here is what constrains the unselectivity of adverbs of quantification.

The paraphrase in (3.c) also indicates unselective binding, though here there is no explicit quantifier providing the universal force. In order to account for this, Lewis in effect assumed that, in the absence of an explicit quantifier, a universal quantifier is supplied by default in the logical translation: I will often refer to this as an implicit default universal quantifier. This default universal interpretation has been convincingly argued by Heim (1982) to derive from the semantics of conditional sentences, and is thus independent of the interpretation of indefinites. The basic idea, following work of Kratzer, *e.g.* (1981), is that *if/then*-sentences, such as (2.c), quite generally are interpreted as involving conditional necessity, and it is from the necessity operator that the universal force derives. Since the main points of this study can be stated in strictly extensional terms, I prefer to avoid introducing the technical complications needed to analyse modality and will stick to using simply a default universal quantifer.

Another kind of default quantifier has been proposed for sentences such as the following:

(6)   Dogs have four legs.

This is usually taken not to be about all dogs whatsoever, but something like all normal dogs, *i.e.*, it wouldn't be falsified by the existence of some three-legged dogs, for example. The implicit quantifier here is said to have generic force. The examples of default quantification I will be discussing mostly involve the universal quantifier, but occasionally there will be instances that might be better treated as involving generic quantification; for the most part, however, I will not bother to carefully distinguish between them. (For detailed discussion of generic quantification, see *e.g.* Carlson (1977), Farkas and Sugioka (1983), and especially Wilkinson (1991).)

These are the observations, relevant to the concerns of this study, that the LHK theory of indefinite quantification is designed to account for; I turn now to the formal details of that account.

2.2 Formulation

The LHK theory is formulated in terms of the theory of restricted quantification. A restricted quantifier can be thought of as a dyadic quantifier whose first argument, the restrictive term, establishes the domain of quantification, so that only substitution-values for the free variables in the restrictive term play a role in evaluating the quantification.[6] For example, suppose the sentence *An honest student rarely cheats.* is interpreted as a restricted quantification with the following logical representation:[7]

(7) $\text{FEW}(x)[\text{honest-student}'(x)][\text{cheat}'(x)]$

The sentence is true, roughly speaking, if and only if for few value-assignments to the free variable x that make the restrictive term (the first bracketed clause) true is there an assignment that makes the second term, which I will follow Heim in calling the nuclear scope, true. (If the restrictive term is not satisfied by the requisite quantity (either absolute or proportional) of assignments, the sentence will either be false or lack a truthvalue, depending on the overall semantic theory employed; I will consider only positive truth conditions, hence leave this choice open.)

An advantage to using restricted quantification for analysing quantified sentences is its ability to model quantifications that are not definable within the standard (*i.e.* bivalent) first-order predicate calculus with truthfunctional connectives, including those involving quantifiers such as MOST, MANY, and FEW (*cf.* Rescher (1962), Platts (1979),

Barwise and Cooper (1981), and especially Westerståhl (1989) for discussion and various proofs). These quantifiers are inherently relational, since they compare the cardinality of a subset of the universe with that of another subset. Such a comparison is easily expressed as a restricted quantification, since the first argument of a restricted quantifier defines one subset and the second argument another. It is of course also straightforward to express universal and existential quantification by means of restricted quantification—by making the first argument a subset of the second, and by making the intersection of the two arguments nonempty, respectively. This relational quality of quantification in general is captured in the theory of generalized quantifiers (*cf.* Mostowski (1957) and Lindström (1966) for the original logical work, and Westerståhl (1989) for an overview). In many respects, the choice between generalized and restricted quantifiers may simply be a matter of point of view: Kratzer (1986), for example, assigns the latter to 'representational' approaches to quantification and the former to 'interpretational' frameworks according as an intermediate level of representation between the syntax and the modeltheoretic interpretation is or is not assumed. The LHK theory has been developed within the representational tradition, and I will pursue that course in this study. (See Chierchia (1988, 1990) and Schwarzschild (1989) for analyses of adverbs of quantification as generalized quantifiers.)

One of the chief tasks of the linguistic use of restrictive quantification is to determine what constitutes the restrictive term in a natural language utterance involving quantification. A number of observations and proposals have been made for deriving the restrictive term, some of which I will discuss in later chapters, one in particular playing a crucial role in my analysis. But for the time being, let us use intuition to get at the appropriate logical representations. Thus, based on the meanings represented by the paraphrases in (3), the sentences in (2) may be given the following respective logical translations on the LHK theory (I have considerably simplified things for present purposes; in particular, I ignore the temporal relations between (what translate as) the restrictive terms and nuclear scopes in (2.b,d)):

(8) a. MOST[quadratic-equation$'(x)$][have-two-different-solutions$'(x)$]

   b. FEW[rider-on-the-13th-Ave-line$'(x)$][seat$'(y)$ & find$'(x,y)$]

    c.   ALL[farmer'(x) & donkey'(y) & own'(x,y)][take-good-care-of'(x,y)]

    d.   MANY[graduate-student'(x) & paper'(y) & submit-to-*LI*'(x,y)][be-rejected'(y)]

We can see how these representations reflect some of the points mentioned in section 2.1 that the theory wants to take into account. In particular, it is only the variables in the restrictive terms that are to get quantified: thus x in (8.b) will, but y will not, be quantified by FEW. The unselectivity of adverbs of quantification is also represented: both x and y in both (8.c) and (8.d) get quantified by the respective adverbs. Moreover, it is now apparent what the constraint on unselectivity is: only and all those variables that are free in the restrictive term of a quantifier are quantified by it (of course, this characterization presupposes a wellformed notion of restrictive term).[8] Finally, the default implicit universal quantifier is represented by ALL in (8.c).

    Although the main features of the LHK theory should now be fairly clear, it may still be worthwhile to recapitulate them in a more general and formal way. The following is my own version of a standard formulation of the semantics of restricted quantification; similar versions can be found in Kamp (1981) and Heim (1982), though they give explicit rules only for universal quantification (in fact, my more general formulation is really a schema for the logical representation and evaluation, not a single rule; a similar general formulation, though expressed in terms of generalized quantifiers, is given in Kamp and Reyle (1990)). I first introduce some notational conventions, then give the general logical representation for restricted quantification in (9), followed by the truth definition in (10). A few clarificatory comments follow the definition.

    Let Ω stand for the translation of an adverb of quantification, ρ and v for (conjunctions of) open sentences of the translation language. Let g be an individual variable assignment, *i.e.*, a function from individual variables to individuals (primed gs are also assignments); let $g' \approx_\varphi g$ mean that $g' = g$ except possibly on the values assigned to the variables free in φ. Finally, define an extensional model M to be an ordered pair $\langle A, \|\cdot\| \rangle$, where A is a nonempty set (of individuals) and $\|\cdot\|$ is the interpretation function, which assigns semantic values to the nonlogical constants of the translation language; $\|\alpha\|^{M,g}$ denotes the semantic value of an arbitrary expression α of the translation language relative to the model *M* and an assignment *g*. Then the general logical representation for restricted quantification is schematized by the formula in (9), which is evaluated according to the rule in (10).

(9) $\Omega[\rho][\nu]$

(10) Where *g* is a variable assignment that assigns values only to the variables that are free in ρ and ν, $\|\Omega[\rho][\nu]\|^{M,g}$ is true iff for Ω-many assignments $g' \approx_{\rho} g$ such that $\|\rho\|^{M,g'}$ is true, there is an assignment $g'' \approx_{\nu-\rho} g'$ such that $\|\nu\|^{M,g''}$ is true.

The proviso that *g* in (10) assign values only to the variables that are free in ρ and ν is needed to avoid the consequences of having to take all variables (of which there are infinitely many) into account: while innocuous with the universal and existential quantifiers, it is semantical-ly detrimental with a quantifier such as MOST, for example (as pointed out *e.g.* by Lewis (1975)), since there is no sense in trying to deter-mine the majority of an infinite number of assignments. But if we only have to consider assignments to the free variables in the formula being evaluated, such a difficulty won't arise (unless the domain itself is infinite in extension, but such cases, say involving numbers, have no general linguistic relevance). In addition, as noted above, (10) is a schema for the interpretation of restricted quantification, with the clause 'Ω-many assignments' standing proxy for the statement of specific cardinalities or proportions, which have distinct definitions (*e.g.* 'most' might be 'more than half').

Note that the final clause in (10), which introduces g'', is an existential statement; since g'' is the assignment function for the nucle-ar scope of the quantifier, this is the source of the existential inter-pretation of indefinites, the variable of whose translation is free in the nuclear scope, such as that of *seats* in (8.b). This is the semantic effect of what Heim (1982) called existential closure of the nuclear scope.[9] It is in order to avoid existentially quantifying the variables that are free in both the restrictive term and the nuclear scope that I have specified that $g'' \approx_{\nu-\rho} g'$: *i.e.*, g'' assigns values only to those variables free in ν that do not occur in ρ;[10] this accounts for the interpretation of senten-ces such as (2.d), with the translation (8.d). (This sort of stipulation can be avoided by building into the truth definition an algorithm that selects the variables to be quantified; see Heim (1982, chapter III) for such a procedure. For present purposes, I prefer to refrain from introducing this additional technical complication.)

A final comment on (9) and (10) concerns the stipulation that ρ and ν be open sentences. This is a concesssion to an apparent fact of natural language, namely, that it does not permit structures in which a quantifier is vacuous, *i.e.*, fails to bind a variable. In terms of restricted quantification, the prohibition must apply to both the restrictive term and the nuclear scope, *i.e.*, the quantifier must bind at least one variable in each of these clauses (this understanding of the constraint is proposed by Kratzer (1989)). In order to insure this, in fact, not only must both ρ and ν be open sentences, in addition the intersection of the sets of free variables they respectively contain must be nonnull. This prohibition is informally stated in (11) (following Kratzer):

(11)   Prohibition against vacuous quantification: in a logical translation of the form in (9), there must be a free occurrence of the same variable in both ρ and ν.

Adverbs of quantification can often be understood as strictly temporal quantifiers, with a frequency reading, and this frequently makes it difficult to see the effect of (11), because a variable over temporal intervals will in such cases be part of the logical representation, precluding a violation of this prohibition. But there are sentences where a frequency reading is excluded or at best strained, and if there is no other element in the sentence that could contain a free variable in the logical representation, it will be ruled out by (11). As an example, compare the following sentence with (2.a):

(12)   The quadratic equation $4x^2 + 15x + 9 = 0$ usually has two different solutions.

The definite subject here cannot be quantified by the adverb of quantification, leaving only the possibility of a frequency reading to avoid a violation of the prohibition against vacuous quantification, but such a reading is semantically implausible due to the properties of the lexical items in the sentence. In the absence of a frequency reading, then, (12) stands in violation of (11).

3 Summary

The major points of the LHK theory are the following: the logical translation of indefinites contains an essentially free variable, that is, it is not inherently bound by a particular quantifier, but may in principle be bound by any quantifier with scope over it; natural language quantifiers have a restrictive term, which determines the domain of quantification; all variables that are free in the restrictive term are quantified by the same quantifier, which is in this respect unselective; variables that are free in the nuclear scope but not in the restrictive term of a quantifier receive existential force. In chapter III I will apply this theory to the analysis of *wh*-clauses; but first, it will be useful to examine how questions, which include some *wh*-clauses (*i.e.* direct and indirect questions), have been semantically analysed in truthconditional terms: this is the topic of the next chapter.

Notes

1. I do not analyse restrictive or appositive relative clauses, though I think they could probably be brought into the general form of my analysis through the semantics of their heads, on which they are in any case semantically dependent. I do, however, briefly treat free (headless) relatives and compare them with quantificational indirect questions.

2. I will for the most part ignore the singular/plural distinction in this study, giving the same kind of open sentence translation for both. In appendix B, however, I comment briefly on this distinction as it affects *wh*-phrases. *Cf.* also chapter III, note 5.

3. I do not treat the effect of definiteness in the body of this study; but I briefly consider, in appendix B, how to incorporate it into my analysis.

4. Lewis considered various possibilities as to what sorts of entities adverbs of quantification quantify over, among them individuals, times, events, and so on. I will in this study largely stick with individual variables, though in certain examples I use a rough and ready temporal variable, and in chapter IV, section 2, I give a brief nod to the possibility of quantifying over situations.

5. As Heim points out (1982, 128*f*.), the way Lewis suggests generating logical forms for such sentences might be compatible with analyzing indefinites as existentially quantified, though the procedure would be considerably more complicated than the variable treatment. Kamp (1981) also analyzes indefinites as open sentences, though his motivation is more from the anaphoric, rather than quantificational, behavior of indefinites (also taken into account by Lewis and Heim). (Kamp and Reyle (1990) is the fullest presentation of this theory to date, and also incorporates a variety of quantifiers, though adverbs of quantification are not treated.)

6. The logical theory of restricted quantification along these lines is developed in Hailperin (1957); an early natural language application is made by Bacon (1965); early incorporations of it into explicit linguistic analyses are in Kasher (1973) and Hausser (1976). See also Altham and Tennant (1975), which specifically treats non-first-orderizable quantifiers such as MOST and also encompasses adverbs of quantification.

7. I use predicate-calculus-style notation, rather than the Discourse Representation Structures of Kamp (1981) or Kamp and Reyle (1990), or Files of Heim (1982), mainly for compactness; all these representations are essentially semantically equivalent. Heim also gives rules for generating Logical Forms from syntactic phrase-structure trees. In chapter V, where I will be more concerned with the relation to surface syntactic representation, I will use tree-structure LF representations as well, and discuss their relation to these logical translations.

8. This expression of the constraint is almost certainly too weak, since it seems that not all variables that are free in the restrictive term are always bound by the quantifier. What is at issue here is what has come to be known as the proportion problem for restricted quantification. A large amount of literature has been devoted in recent years to this issue, with a number of different proposals for dealing with it; see Kratzer (1989) for references and what I consider a promising approach to the topic. The proportion problem is essentially orthogonal to the main concerns of this study, so I do not feel overly negligent in ignoring it here.

9. Kamp (1981) suggested having it be part of the truth definition, rather than explicitly having an existential quantifier in the logical representation; this seems reasonable, since existential closure is confined to the nuclear scope, and therefore is conceptually quite different from the restricted quantification that natural language otherwise exhibits.

10. If there are no free variables unique to p, *i.e.*, the variables in p-v constitute a subset of those in v, then $g'' = g'$.

II

An Overview of Semantic Analyses of Questions

1 Introduction

In this chapter I review several semantic analyses of questions. My purpose is to provide the background against which my own analysis, within the LHK theory laid out in chapter I, will stand in contrast; therefore the scope of my review here is rather limited—in fact, I will essentially confine it to certain aspects of the truthconditional meaning of questions. I do this because I am not attempting in this study to analyse the illocutionary act of interrogation, but rather the quantificational properties of sentences, some of which can be used to produce this speech act; and truthconditional semantics is well-suited to treating quantification. As the analyses I will review amply illustrate, it is quite plausible to associate questions with truth conditions, and doing so allows their incorporation into semantic theories of declarative sentences, which are standardly given a truthconditional analysis.

Since the basic truthvalue-bearing unit is the proposition, giving a truthconditional analysis of questions entails associating them in some way with propositions. As we will see, there are quite a few ways of making this association, but they can be grouped into three general conceptual approaches, which I will refer to as the categorial, the embedding, and the propositional approaches.[1] On the categorial approach (section 2) the denotation of a question combines with that of its characteristic answer to yield a proposition; on embedding analyses (section 3), questions are treated as compound declarative sentences, which denote propositions; on the propositional approach, question-denotations are associated more directly propositions, either by identifying them with sets of propositions (section 4.1) or with propositions themselves (section 4.2).

My review concentrates on how these approaches provide truthconditional semantics to questions, particularly *wh*-questions and *yes/no*-questions (*e.g.*, *Who left?* and *Do you want coffee?*; I will not deal substantively with alternative questions, *e.g. Do you want coffee or tea?*). I will also review how the approaches handle indirect questions, *e.g. John knows who left*.[2] In addition, I will consider how the approaches fare with respect to the question-counterparts of a couple of what I take to be fairly standard adequacy tests for truthconditional semantic theories, namely, the ability to handle coordination and the entailment from a conjoined sentence to each of its conjuncts.[3]

This chapter does not constitute an exhaustive review of the literature, even in the limited domain I am concerned with; but within that domain, I do consider what I believe to be the best-known and most influential recent treatments. More comprehensive surveys of semantic analyses of questions may be found in Groenendijk and Stokhof—henceforth G&S—(1984, ch.I) and Bäuerle and Zimmermann (1987), to both of which I am heavily indebted for the content of my discussion. For additional critical presentations *cf.* also Egli (1976), Wunderlich (1976), Hirschbühler (1978), Bäuerle (1979), Grewendorf (1983), and Hoepelman (1983); Harrah (1984) surveys more specifically logical issues in the analysis of questions.

2   Categorial Approaches

On the categorial approach the denotation of a question combines with that of its characteristic answer to yield a proposition. In the case of *wh*-questions, the characteristic answer is taken to be a phrase of the same category as the *wh*-phrase; hence the name of this approach. With *yes/no*-questions, the characteristic answers are, of course, *yes* and *no*. Among the exponents of this approach are Keenan and Hull (1973), Egli (1973; 1974; 1976), Hiz (1978a), Hausser and Zaefferer (1979), and Hausser (1983; 1984). A consequence of this approach is that questions themselves have no uniform semantic type, but their type is determined by that of the category with which they combine to produce a proposition. To illustrate, here are a few examples of questions and corresponding characteristic answers; accompanying each pair

are the (intuitively simplest) associated types, which combined give the
type t of a proposition (e is the type of an individual (concept)):

(13)   a.   Who left? John. $\langle e,t \rangle$; e
       b.   When did John leave? Yesterday. $\langle \langle t,t \rangle, t \rangle$; $\langle t,t \rangle$
       c.   Did Mary leave? No. $\langle \langle t,t \rangle, t \rangle$; $\langle t,t \rangle$
       d.   How many books did Mary write? Three.
            $\langle \langle \langle e,t \rangle, \langle \langle e,t \rangle, t \rangle \rangle, t \rangle$; $\langle \langle e,t \rangle, \langle \langle e,t \rangle, t \rangle \rangle$

There are various ways of implementing this type of analysis
within a formal semantic framework. For Keenan and Hull, it is only
the ordered pair of a question and an answer that is truthconditionally
evaluated, so that the question itself has no independent meaning. In
contrast, Egli, Hausser and Zaefferer, and Hausser give questions independent meanings by treating them as λ-expressions, in which the variable
that is abstracted over is the type of the category of a characteristic
answer; this entails that a question denotes a function from a characteristic answer (to that question) to a proposition.

Because on a categorial approach questions come in a number of
semantic types, certain manipulations have to be done into order to
treat coordination. It is usually assumed that coordinated constituents
must be of the same semantic type; given the types associated with the
questions in (13) above, this means that, although (13.b) and (13.c) can
be coordinated, (13.a) and (13.b), for example, cannot, at least on the
simplest categorial analysis: yet a question such as *Who left and when
did Bill arrive?* is unobjectionable. A related difficulty is the entailment
relationship that holds between a conjoined sentence and each of its
conjuncts (*cf.* G&S (1984, ch.I; 1989): for instance, the previous
question entails both the questions *Who left?* and *When did Bill arrive?*,
in the sense that an answer to the conjoined question entails an answer
to both conjunct-questions; but, as with coordination, entailment is
usually taken to hold only between constituents of the same type.

Similar difficulties arise with question embedding:[4] since any
direct question can be embedded under a suitable predicate, the categorial
approach seems to require associating question-embedding predicates
with as many types as there are types of questions, in order to get both
Mary knows who left. and *Mary knows when John left.*, for example.
Moreover, the types would have be further multiplied in view of the
possibility of embedded coordinated questions, as in *Mary knows who*

left and when Bill arrived., also to account for the corresponding entailments. (The same considerations apply to coordination of questions and
declaratives and the fact that certain predicates can embed both questions
and declaratives, the latter being of type *t*.)

Perhaps the only plausible way of dealing with coordination and
embedding in a categorial analysis is to employ typeshifting. This is
the hypothesis that certain constituents are associated not with a single
type, once and for all, but with a family of types, one of which is
taken to be basic, but in appropriate contexts the others will be called
for. This idea has been exploited for the analysis of noun phrases in
Partee (1987), and in fact for questions as well in G&S (1989), though
within a propositional approach. The task for a defender of the categorial approach would be to motivate the necessary typeshifting in a prin-
cipled way, that is, to find a general characterization of the relation
between the types of the questions in (13), for example (whatever those
types might be), that will allow for coordination, and similarly for the
type-relation between questions and question-embedding predicates.

3   Embedding Approaches

The basic idea of embedding approaches is to analyse questions
in terms of a more familiar truthconditional object—declarative sentences. Specifically, all questions are treated as semantically compound
declaratives. There are two well-known versions of this approach, of
which I will just briefly mention one, while devoting the bulk of this
section to the other.

3.1 Lewis (1972)

Lewis (1972) proposed that the meaning of a direct question is
identified with the meaning of a performative utterance in which the
question is embedded. For instance, *Did John leave?* means the same
thing as *I ask you whether John left.*, and the latter is true just in case
the speaker asks the addressee whether John left; similarly with a *wh*-
question such as *Who left?*. Actually, Lewis treats the matrix predicate
as a compound of *ask* and a *wh*-phrase; for example, the above sentences are assigned something like the following respective structures: [$_S$I

[$_\text{VP}$ask-whether you [$_\text{S}$John left]]] and [$_\text{S}$I [$_\text{VP}$ask-who you [$_\text{VP}$left]]]. Notice that this makes the "rest" of the question, minus the *wh*-phrase, consist of categorially different consituents, just like on the categorial analysis. Thus this analysis will have the same difficulty as the latter with coordination and entailment. In addition, this analysis seems to have nothing to say about indirect questions such as *I know who left.* and *I wonder whether John left.*; the matrix predicates here are not performatives, nor is a performative paraphrase appro-priate for these sentences.[5]

3.2 Åqvist/Hintikka

The other embedding analysis I want to discuss in more detail is due to Åqvist (1965; 1975) and further developed, especially in relation to natural language, by Hintikka (1974; 1976; 1983). There are three distinguishing features of this analysis. One is relevant only to the treatment of direct questions: their logical translation contains two operators, an imperative operator, which may be rendered in English as 'bring it about that' and an epistemic operator, in English 'I know that'; hence, this is often referred to as the imperative-epistemic approach to questions.[6] Secondly, the propositional content of the question is rendered by a declarative, specifically, a *that*-clause, which is embedded under the epistemic operator. For example, the question *Did John leave?* receives a translation that may be paraphrased as in (14):

(14)   Bring it about that if John left then I know that John left and if John didn't leave then I know that John didn't leave.

It is the propositional content that provides the answer to the question; in this case, *e.g.*, that John left or that John didn't leave, whichever is true. The third feature pertains to *wh*-questions: these are treated as quantified sentences, in which the quantifier is either universal or existential. Thus, *Who left?* receives both of the following logical forms (where ! is the imperative and K the epistemic operator; in addition, primed English expressions stand for translations of nonlogi-cal constants (lexical items), a practice I follow throughout this study):

(15)   a. $!\forall x[\text{left}'(x) \rightarrow K(\text{left}'(x))]$
        b. $!\exists x[\text{left}'(x) \wedge K(\text{left}'(x))]$

On the first translation, the question is true if and only if I (as asker) come to know, for each person who left, that he left; it is true on the second translation if and only if I come to know, for some person who left, that he left. Hintikka says that both readings are always available in principle, though in a given context one may be favored. Answers to *wh*-questions are obtained by supplying the appropriate number of substitutions-instances to the free variable(s), yielding propositions.

The application of this analysis to indirect questions is straight-forward, all that is needed is to omit the imperative operator and substitute for the epistemic operator the appropriate matrix verb (also a sentential operator). For example, *Mary found out who left.* has the following two translations:

(16)   a. $\forall x[\text{left}'(x) \rightarrow \text{find-out}'(m,\text{left}'(x))]$
        b. $\exists x[\text{left}'(x) \wedge \text{find-out}'(m,\text{left}'(x))]$

The universal/existential dichotomy in the logical translations is cleary exemplified in some sentences containing an indirect question; consider, for example, the following sentence:

(17)   Mary told John who sells espresso machines.

This sentence is intuitively true in case Mary supplied John with a list of all the places that sell espresso machines (the universal reading), but also if she merely gave him the name of one or two, but not all, such places (the existential reading).

Since what I called above the propositional content of the question is semantically a sentence (*i.e.* the type of a truthvalue-bearing constituent), this analysis has no problem either with coordination of questions or of a question and a declarative, or with embedding. In the case of *wh*-questions, the propositional content is, to be sure, an open sentence, that is, it contains a free variable, but still it is of the appropriate type to conjoin with *yes/no*-questions and declaratives, and to be embedded under a clause-taking predicate. For the same reason, the entailment between a coordinated question and each of its conjuncts is straightforward. It is worth highlighting in this connection a crucial difference between this approach and the categorial approaches using λ-abstraction: although on both approaches the logical core of a *wh*-question is an open sentence, only on the Åqvist/Hintikka analysis is this the locus of coordination and embedding; on the categorial approach the locus is closed formulas, the λ-expressions, and these formulas differ in type. In this respect, the difference between the two approaches comes down to a difference in the scope of binding of the free variables in the question translation: on the categorial approach, the free variables are bound from within the question, as it were, while on the Åqvist/Hintikka embedding approach, the free variables are bound in effect from outside of the question by the quantifier.[7]

A difficulty for the Åqvist/Hintikka analysis concerns question-embedding predicates such as *wonder* and *ask*, which, unlike *know* and *find out*, do not also embed *that*-clauses. For instance, the meaning of the following sentence cannot be paraphrased by 'John wonders that Mary left or that Mary did not leave.'

(18)   John wonders whether Mary left.

To account for this, Hintikka (1976) suggests that "only a verb which idiomatically carries a success presupposition...can naturally" embed a question (p.67). A success presupposition sanctions the entailment from, for example, *John knows who left.* of *For each person who in fact left, John knows that he left.* This is just the universal translation that Hintikka's analysis assigns, so it doesn't really explain why such a translation is unavailable for *wonder*. Moreover, it would seem to rule out the existential reading, which Hintikka showed to be contextually available. A different solution, mentioned by Karttunen (1977) and Boër (1978), would be to decompose the meaning of *wonder* (and that of similar predicates) using a *that*-clause-embedding verb; for example, the meaning of (18) might be paraphrased as in (19) (following Boër):

(19)   John wants, if Mary left, to know that Mary left and, if Mary didn't leave, to know that Mary didn't leave.

Karttunen points out that a similar decompositional treatment does not seem forthcoming for a predicate such as *depend on*, which also fails to embed a *that*-clause in the object position. In response, Boër offers an analysis that involves a relation of counterfactual causation, which he claims answers this objection; I refrain, however, from going into the somewhat abstruse details of Boër's analysis.[8]

4   Propositional Approaches

There are two main subapproaches within the propositional approach to the semantics of questions. According to one, represented most prominently by Hamblin (1976 [1973]) and Karttunen (1977), (but *cf.* also Bennett (1979) and Belnap (1982)), questions denote sets of propositions; according to the other, defended by G&S (1982; 1984; 1989), the denotation of a question is simply a proposition, though differing from the proposition denoted by the corresponding declarative sentence. I will consider these two approaches in turn.

4.1   *Questions as Denoting Sets of Propositions*

4.1.1   *Hamblin (1973)*

Hamblin's analysis is carried out in the logical framework of Montague (1970). It is motivated by the desire to provide a unified treatment within this framework for both indicative and interrogative utterances. Hamblin starts by noting syntactic parallels between *wh*-phrases and noninterrogative phrases of the same syntactic category; he says (1976, 253) *e.g.* that *who* and *what* "are interrogative proper nouns, in the sense that they take the same positions in sentences as proper nouns do." However, the semantics of *wh*-phrases is not the same as the corresponding proper nouns: *who* and *what* do not denote individuals. Rather, Hamblin suggests that they denote sets of individuals. To implement this idea, he introduces the concept of a denotation-set, that is, a set consisting of the denotations of a phrase. For phrases that have just one denotation, their denotation-sets are singletons; *e.g.* the denotation-set of the name *Mary* is just the set containing the individual Mary, {m}. Similarly, the denotation-set of *left* is the unit set containing the usual denotation of this predicate, *i.e.* the set of those who left (to be precise, a function from individuals to propositions, which applied to an individual *a* yields the proposition that *a* left). But for some phrases, in particular *wh*-words and those containing them, their denotation-sets will in general have more than one member.[9]

Hamblin defines an operation by which the application of members of one denotation-set to members of another denotation-set yields a third denotation-set; this is the analogue in terms of denotation-sets of function application.[10] The denotation-set of *Who left?*, for example, is the set of propositions each of which results from applying a member (=the member, in this case) of the denotation-set of *left* to a member of the denotation-set of *who*, *i.e.* the set of propositions {*a* left, *b* left, *c* left,...} for each person *a*, *b*, *c*,... in the domain. The denotation-set of a *yes/no*-question such as *Did John leave?* will be the set containing both the positive and negative propositions corresponding to the question, *e.g.* {John left, John did not leave}. Thus, this analysis captures Hamblin's position regarding the question-answer relation; *cf.* (1976, 254): "Pragmatically speaking a question sets up a choice-situation between a set of propositions, namely, those propositions that count as answers to it." Note that since, in possible-worlds semantics, a proposition is identified with a set of worlds (more precisely, a function from worlds to truthvalues), the denotation-set of a proposition is a set of sets of worlds.

Since questions denote sets of propositions on this analysis, regardless of what kinds of questions they are, they have a single semantic type, so there is no problem as far as coordinating questions is concerned, nor is there difficulty getting the associated entailments, since the denotation-sets of each conjunct are obviously subsets of the denotation-set of the conjoined question. On the other hand, the possibility of coordinating a question and a declarative sentence, as in *I was at the beach today and who do you think I saw?* requires a change in the standard semantics of statements; Hamblin proposes to treat both types of sentences as denoting sets of propositions, the only difference being that the denotation-set of a declarative sentence is a singleton, just as is the denotation-set of a proper name or a verb, as we have seen. Not only does this solve the problem of coordination, it also permits a uniform treatment of predicates that embed both interrogative and declarative clauses: they will simply take objects that denote sets of propositions (Hamblin does not actually consider indirect questions in his presentation). As an alternative to saying that declarative sentences (as well as subsentential noninterrogative constituents) have singleton sets as denotations, it might be possible to invoke typeshifting, as was suggested for the categorial analysis of questions. On Hamblin's analysis, however, it is not questions or *wh*-phrases whose type would shift, but declaratives and other noninterrogative phrases.

4.1.2 Karttunen (1977)

Hamblin's fundamental approach to questions was taken up by Karttunen (1977) within the framework of Montague (1973).[11] Karttunen claimed that there is a basic difference between the two in that on his analysis questions denote sets of propositions that are true answers, not all possible answers, to them. (More accurately, Karttunen's analysis yields sets of all true propositions that correspond to the question or else, if there are no such true propositions, the empty set.[12]) But, as noted by G&S (1984, ch.I, n.38), there is really no substantive difference: since Hamblin's denotation-set for a proposition is a set of sets of worlds, it is a straightforward matter to single out, at any world w_i, the propositions which are true at w_i: simply collect together the subsets of the denotation-set of which w_i is a member. So for a given question evaluated at a given index, Hamblin's and Karttunen's analyses yield the same set of propositions.[13]

Karttunen's reason for wanting only true propositions to be in the denotation of a question is the observation that, under certain predicates, indirect questions are apparently only understood as denoting true propositions, even though *that*-clauses under the same predicate (when possible) may not be true; the following examples from Karttunen (his (18) and (19.b), respectively) illustrate this:

(20) a. Who is elected depends on who is running.
      b. John told Mary who passed the test.

In (20.a) the relation of dependency is between people who in fact are elected and people who in fact are running, not any possible people. Similarly, in (20.b) it seems that John cannot have told Mary *e.g.* that Bill passed the test if in fact Bill did not pass the test. (This observation was to my knowledge first pointed out by Baker (1968, 83-84).)[14] But again, if we form the denotation-sets of these sentences à la Hamblin, then at any index of evaluation we get only those propositions that are true at that index. In other words, although Karttunen builds into his translation procedure the requirement that only true propositions be allowed in the denotation of a question, this does not seem to be strictly necessary, given that truth is in any case index-dependent (for contingent propositions).

Moreover, the insistence on true propositions appears to yield wrong results in some cases. Thus, although Karttunen says (1977, 11) that "[t]he same point can be made with regard to other question embedding verbs such as *be interested in*, *investigate*, *wonder*, etc.," yet it seems to me that the truth entailment observed in (20) does not hold in the following sentence:

(21)   John wonders who left.

I find it equally odd to say that this sentence means that John stands in the wondering relation either to the set of true propositions of the form ⌐x left⌐ or to the empty set, the only two possibilities on Karttunen's analysis. But it seems plausible to say that (21) places John in the wondering relation to the set of all propositions, true or false, of the form ⌐x left⌐, which would be the result on Hamblin's analysis if we assume that the value of the complement of *wonder* is not tied to a particular index; at least Hamblin's analysis is not inconsistent with this assumption, but Karttunen's is. (This is basically the approach of Boër (*cf.* (19) in section 3 above: *want* introduces intensionality) and of G&S, discussed in below in section 4.2; I return to question-embedding under verbs such as *wonder* also in chapter III, section 4.1.)

While Karttunen represents his analysis as associating questions with the set of their true answers when contrasting his approach with Hamblin's (*cf.* (1977, 10): "I choose to make questions denote the set of propositions expressed by their true answers instead of the set of propositions expressed by their possible answers."), his conception of the question-answer relation is more restrictive than this suggests. He does not consider each proposition in the set to be a true and complete answer to the question; rather, he says (p.20) that "the propositions in this set jointly consitute a [*sic*] true and complete answer to the question." In other words, Karttunen considers a question to have at most one complete true answer at an index (or none, if it denotes the empty set); the individual propositions in the denotation are at best partial true answers (unless of course the denotation is a singleton).[15] Contrasting with this conception is that of Bennett and Belnap (*cf.* Bennett (1979) and Belnap (1982)), according to which questions also denote sets of propositions, each of which, however, itself counts as a complete true answer to the question. The following example (from G&S (1984, ch.I(17))) is a case in point:

(22)   What did two of John's friends give him for Christmas?

One complete true answer might be: *Two of John's friends, quite coincidentally, gave him the latest Jan Garbarek CD for Christmas*; another complete true answer might be: *Bill gave him the latest Jan Garbarek CD and Mary gave him an electric coffee mill*. Evidently, the question in (22) is ambiguous: on the reading for which the first answer is appropriate, the *wh*-phrase has scope over the indefinite subject, on the reading for which the second answer is appropriate, the scopes are reversed. In fact, because of this ambiguity, (22) is not really a counterexample to Karttunen's claim about complete true answers, since it could be plausibly argued that this one string of words actually stands for two questions, having distinct logical representations and therefore distinct semantic interpretations—this is indeed Karttunen's position (*cf.* (1977, 32*f.*) and his example (69)).[16]

On the other hand, it appears that Karttunen's theory is truly contradicted by sentences such as (17), repeated here:

(17)   Mary told John who sells espresso machines.

As we saw, this is ambiguous between a reading on which Mary informed John of all the dealers in espresso machines and one on which she only told him of some; for examples, (17) is true if Mary told John that the Coffee Gallery sells espresso machines (and this is true), even if this isn't the only store that sells espresso machines. But it is only the former reading that Karttunen's analysis yields. Notice that on both readings the *wh*-phrase has scope over the indefinite object (since Mary need have no particular espresso machines in mind), showing that this is not a case of scope ambiguity, as in (22). That sentences such as (17) have the latter reading, which G&S (1984, ch.VI) call the mention-some reading, seems to be striking counterevidence to an analysis, such as Karttunen's, which permits questions to have only one true complete answer (at an index of evaluation). It is perhaps somewhat surprising, in view of this, that G&S themselves present such an analysis, which I discuss in the next subsection, though, as we will see, they propose a way of incorporating the mention-some reading into it.

4.2 Questions as Denoting Propositions—Groenendijk and Stokhof (1982)

If Karttunen's intention that each question has at most one true complete answer is combined with his treatment of questions as denoting sets of propositions, then these sets should never be more than singletons; yet Karttunen's formal analysis still in general delivers multimembered sets of propositions. [17] The possible-worlds treatment of G&S (1982; 1984; 1989) builds the one-true-answer conception right into its semantics, by making questions denote, not singleton sets of propositions, but simply propositions. An immediate consequence of this is that nothing need be done to sanction coordination of questions and declaratives, since both are taken to denote propositions (the latter standardly so); and clearly the associated entailments are straightforward, as well. In addition, other things being equal, it is expected that predicates that embed *that*-clauses should also embed questions, and vice versa (since this expectation is in fact not always met, other things are not equal and remain to be explained, but this is so for all analyses). As we have seen, both categorial analyses and those that treat questions as denoting sets of propositions can accommodate these facts only by either multiplying lexical entries, appealing to typeshifting, or (on the latter approaches) making declaratives denotes singleton-sets of propositions.

Of course, the propositions that questions are to denote must be distinguished from those that declaratives denote, since these two types of sentences do not mean the same thing. The need for a distinction is especially clear from the possibility of embedding either clause-type under the same predicate, as in *John knows who was at the party* and *John knows that Mary was at the party*, assuming that the matrix predicate has the same meaning in both cases. What G&S do is to make the denotation of a question depend on the index at which it is evaluated (*cf.* also Lewis (1982) for a similar treatment of *whether*-clauses); that is, unlike a declarative, which denotes the same proposition at any index, what proposition a question denotes varies, in general, from index to index. For example, *Mary likes John* denotes that proposition (more accurately, that function from indices to truthvalues) which, at a given index, is true if and only if at that index Mary likes John; in effect, it denotes the set of indices at which Mary likes John. In contrast, *Does Mary like John?* denotes that proposition which, at a given index, is true if and only if for any index k, the truthvalue of the proposition that Mary likes John is the same at k as at the given index. By convention, the given index is usually taken to be the real (actual) world, so that the denotation of the previous question is just whatever proposition is the case in the real world, either that Mary likes John or that Mary doesn't like John. For a *wh*-question such as *Who does Mary like?*, the proposition it denotes at the real world is true if and only if for any index k, the people Mary likes at k are the same as those she likes at the real world. Since this proposition includes all and only the people Mary likes at the real world, it clearly constitutes a true complete answer to the question, and the formal properties of G&S's semantics have the consequence that it is the only true complete answer at that index.[18]

I noted in the previous subsection that Karttunen's analysis yields an intuitively wrong account of sentences such as (21) (*John wonders who left*), since it seems odd to say that John is in the wondering relation either to the set of true propositions saying who left (*i.e.* to the set of leavers) or to the empty set. G&S agree with this intuition, and their account of it runs as follows. As a rule, embedding shifts the context of evaluation, so that, in particular, the index or world with respect to which an embedded clause is evaluated is different from that with respect to which the matrix clause is evaluated. In the case of (21), this has the effect that the proposition denoted by *who left* need not be true at the world at which it is true that John wonders about something (*e.g.* the real world)—in other words, the proposition John stands in the wondering relation to need not (and in general will not) be about those who actually left. In contrast, with a sentence such as *John knows who left*, we do intuitively want John to stand in the knowing relation to those who actually left; G&S accomplish this by making *know* subject to a meaning postulate that removes the usual index-shifting effect of embedding, so that that in this case the index of evaluation is the same for both matrix and embedded clause. G&S term verbs such as *know*, which are subject to this meaning postulate, extensional predicates, and those such as *wonder*, which are not subject to the postulate, intensional predicates.[19]

I have already noted, and G&S are aware of, the existence of sentences that evidently have more than one true complete answer at an index; these are what they call sentences with mention-some readings, exemplified by the sentence in (17). G&S (1984, 534*ff.*) propose to incorporate these cases into their basic treatment by analysing them not as single questions but as disjunctions of questions, and allowing an answer to at least one of the disjuncts to count as a complete answer to the original question itself (at the index of evaluation). For example, *Who sells espresso machines?* on its mention-some reading is semantically equivalent to *Does* a *sell espresso machines or does* b *sell espresso machines or does* c *sell espresso machines or...?*, for each individual *a*, *b*, *c*,... in the domain, and the (true) answer '*a* sells espresso machines' will count as complete even if there are others who sell espresso machines. (If there is no one who sells espresso machines, G&S regard the mention-some reading as false.) In the case of an indirect question under an extensional predicate, as in (17) (*tell*, like *know*, is extensional, according to G&S), the result will be the proposition that for someone who in fact sells espresso machines, Mary told John that he sells espresso machines. Note that this is just the existential reading produced on the Åqvist/Hintikka analysis. With an intensional predicate such as *wonder*, there is no entailment that there is someone who sells espresso machines on the mention-some reading of the following sentence:

(23) John wonders who sells espresso machines.

G&S claim that this reading is distinct from the normal 'mention-all' reading in that, if wondering entails not knowing, then the mention-some reading of (23) entails that for no one who sells espresso machines does John know that he sells espresso machines, while on its mention-all reading (23) entails only that not for everyone who sells espresso machines does John know that he sells espresso machines. I do not find the latter entailment forthcoming without an explicit indication that there are some people of whom John knows that they sell espresso machines, as in the following:

(24) (Although he knows that the Coffee Gallery sells espresso machines,) John wonders who else sells espresso machines.

5 Summary

I have reviewed in this chapter a variety of truthconditional approaches to the semantics of questions. They exhibit a sort of progression in terms of empirical coverage. The categorial approaches have prima facie difficulty with coordination and the associated entailments, as well as with embedding, because of the nonuniformity of the semantic types associated with questions. The Åqvist/Hintikka approach handles coordination and certain cases of embedding, but has difficulties with other cases, involving verbs such as *wonder* and *ask*. The propositional approaches deal with these, but at least those of Karttunen and G&S, which make questions denote one true complete answer at an index, lose the universal/existential ambiguity captured handily on the Åqvist/Hintikka account. G&S, it is true, introduce additional meaning rules to capture this ambiguity, but once it is admitted that questions can have interpretations on which they don't have just one true complete answer, the question arises whether it is possible to give an adequate analysis according to which this is the general interpretation of questions, in effect, a return to the intuitions behind both the Åqvist/Hintikka and the Hamblin accounts, but overcoming some of their inadequacies. In the rest of this study, this is what I attempt to do. My analysis consists of a generalization of the Åqvist/Hintikka approach for certain question-constructions, plus a version of the Hamblin approach for others, carried out within the basic assumptions of the LHK theory of quantification summarized in chapter I. A consequence of my analysis is that the class of question constructions divides into two logicosemantically distinct types, and much of the empirical effort of this study is directed towards supporting this division.

Notes

1. The labels 'categorial' and 'propositional' have been employed by Bäuerle (1979), Kiefer (introduction to 1983), and Groenendijk and Stokhof (1984, ch.I; 1989). Bäuerle and Zimmermann (1987) use the term 'Reduktionstheorien' to characterize what I am calling embedding approaches.

2. Throughout this chapter I the employ the term 'indirect question' to refer to sentences of the kind illustrated in the text. As will become clear in chapter III, however, my own analysis divides these constructions into two logicosemantically distinct types, based on their quantificational behavior. But since the evidence for this distinction does not play an essential role in my review of other analyses, which do not make this distinction, I retain the traditional designation for the time being.

3. I will not, however, consider in this chapter a certain entailment relation proposed by G&S (1984, chapter I), namely that from *Who left?* to *Did John leave?*. This does not at all seem to me an intuitively obvious entailment, in the way that the entailment of the conjuncts from a conjunction is. It is, however, a consequence of G&S's theory, which my analysis argues against. I return in chapter IV to the issue involved in this entailment (namely, strong exhaustiveness), as it applies to indirect questions.

4. The only categorial analysis of indirect questions that I know of is Hull (1975), which, however, only considers a small class of indirect *wh*-questions; an analysis in terms of λ-expressions would seem to have wider application, though it would face the problems mentioned in the text.

5. The use of a performative paraphrase for direct questions is not tied to Lewis's compounding of *ask* and a *wh*-phrase; in particular, Karttunen (1977) proposes that direct questions are analysed as indirect questions, which on his analysis are interpreted as sets of propositions (see section 4.1.2 below), embedded under a performative such as 'I ask you to tell me.' On this analysis, coordination of questions and entailments between them are unproblematic.

6. These operators are primitives of a formal calculus, and are given modeltheoretic intepretations in accordance with the theory of them developed by Hintikka (*e.g.* 1962). This is basically a kind of

intensional semantics, where truth is made relative to sets of suitable (imperative and epistemic) alternative possibilities.

7. The variable-binding could also be done by λ-abstraction, given that, e.g., $\forall x[\phi(x) \to \psi(x)]$ is equivalent to $\forall[\lambda x[\phi(x) \to \psi(x)]]$; in the latter, the quantifier is simply treated as a predicate, of the type of a generalized quantifier, and does not also do service as a variable-binder. The point remains that the binding is outside the scope of the *wh*-clause itself. (Thanks to Ede Zimmermann for helpful discussion of these points.)

8. Boër presents an analysis of indirect questions in which the embedded constituent is treated as the category of a nominal. Since all questions are of this category, as well as embedded declaratives (*i.e.*, *that*-clauses), there is no problem with coordination or entailment. His analysis, which is formulated in terms of Cresswell's (1973) λ-categorial semantics, yields meanings for questions that, like Hintikka's, correspond to those of propositions denoted by *that*-clauses, raising similar problems as for Hintikka's analysis—this is why Boër appeals to decomposition and various other technical maneuvers. However, his analysis only produces meanings corresponding to Hintikka's universal reading, not also the existential one; therefore, it predicts no ambiguity in a sentence such as (5). In addition, Boër does not intend his analysis to apply to direct questions. Von Stechow (1989) presents a simpler version of Boër's analysis in terms of both the two-dimensional semantics developed for focus constructions by Rooth (1985) as well as the structured meanings approach (*cf.* Cresswell (1985)).

9. Hamblin does not specify whether there is a general way to determine if the denotation-set of a given phrase is a unit set or has multiple members; though he does distinguish interrogative from indicative categories, perhaps suggesting a lexically marked distinction.

10. The set-theoretic definition of this operation is: $\alpha```\beta = \{\gamma: \exists a \in \alpha \exists b \in \beta[\gamma = a(b)]\}$ (Hamblin (1976, 255)).

11. Karttunen actually intends this analysis to apply to indirect questions only, not also direct questions as on Hamblin's analysis. For the latter, Karttunen suggests that they should be treated as indirect questions embedded under a performative verb expressing the interrogative speech act (*cf.* note 5 above).

12. The basis of Karttunen's analysis is the intensional logic formula in (i), the IL translation of what he calls a 'proto-question':

(i) $\lambda p[{}^\lor p \land p = {}^\land \varphi]$

p is a variable over propositions and φ is the translation of a sentence. Karttunen treat *wh*-NPs as existentially quantified NPs, which are quantified into (i); thus the translation of *Who left?* is as in (ii):

(ii) $\lambda p \exists x[{}^\lor p \land p = {}^\land \text{left}'(x)]$

Yes/no-questions are treated as alternative questions; the translation of *Did John leave?* reduces to the formula in (iii):

(iii) $\lambda p[{}^\lor p \land [p = {}^\land \text{left}'(j) \lor p = {}^\land \neg \text{left}'(j)]]$

If the negative disjunct were left out, then if John did not leave, the analysis would deliver the empty set, obviously not what is wanted.

13. While it is always possible to get true propositions on Hamblin's analysis, Karttunen's cannot always reconstruct a Hamblinesque denotation-set. By taking the union of the set of true propositions over the set of worlds, Karttunen's analysis delivers a set of sets of worlds of which any world is a member, but it lacks the empty set. In other words, Hamblin allows the necessarily false proposition to be a possible answer, but Karttunen does not.

14. In addition, sentences such as (8.b) have been claimed to entail that for every person who passed the test, John told Mary that that person passed the test; this is the judgment of Baker and Karttunen, as well as Boër (*cf.* note 8). A problem for this claim is posed by the ambiguity of the sentence in (17) above. I comment further on this directly below, and take up the issue again in detail in chapter IV.

15. The question-answer relation is notoriously slippery, because what counts as an answer to a given question evidently depends in large part on the context in which the question is asked. But it seems in general possible to isolate purely semantic properties of the question-answer relation, that abstract away from context and contextual appropriateness. It is with respect to the semantics of the question-answer relation that Karttunen's claim is intended. The same holds for the other analyses I discuss. For discussion of the semantics and pragmatics of the question-answer relation, *cf.* Baker (1968, ch.III), and especially Grewendorf (1983) and G&S (1984, chs.IV-V).

16. Karttunen's semantic rules in fact yield the reading where the indefinite has scope over the *wh*-phrase only on the assumption that direct questions are semantically the same as indirect questions, where the embedding predicate is a kind of performative verb expressing interrogativity (*cf.* note 11). Because Karttunen's analysis does not allow quantifying into question-translations, it does not get one of the readings of a sentence such as the following (as pointed out by Bennett (1977)):

(i)   John wonders where two unicorns live.

The missing reading is the one where the indefinite has scope over the *wh*-phrase but under the matrix predicate. This shortcoming of Karttunen (1977) was remedied in Karttunen and Peters (1980).

17. At an index of evaluation, for *yes/no*-questions, the set will always be either a singleton or else empty; for alternative questions with *n* alternatives, the set will contain at most *n* propositions; for *wh*-questions, the set will contain as many propositions as there are substitution-values for the *wh*-phrase(s) that yield true propositions. A singleton could, of course, be obtained from a nonsingleton set delivered by Karttunen's semantics by forming the intersection of the set: this would amount to the conjunction of all the propositions in the previous set.

18. G&S implement their account in the language of two-sorted type-theory (Ty2; *cf.* Gallin (1975)), which contains variables over indices, which can hence be quantified and abstracted over. (However, Zimmermann (1985) showed that G&S's semantics for questions can be carried out in the intensional logic of Montague (1973), which is slightly weaker than Ty2—though, as Zimmermann (1989) showed, the difference between the two is irrelevant for linguistic applications.) The Ty2 translation of *Does Mary like John?* is the following:

(i) $\lambda i[\text{like}'(a)(m,j) = \text{like}'(i)(m,j)]$

The variable *a* represents the real world, and its being free guarantees that the proposition (set of indices *i*) that (i) denotes depends on what is the case at the real world. For *wh*-questions, the *wh*-phrase is treated syncategorematically, translating as a λ-abstracted predicate over individuals. The translation of *Who does Mary like?* is thus as follows:

(ii) $\lambda i[\lambda x[\text{like}'(a)(\text{m},x)] = \lambda x[\text{like}'(i)(\text{m},x)]]$

To get the sense of a question, the free index-variable is abstracted over, producing a formula that expresses a relation between indices. This is in fact an equivalence relation on the set of indices, which means that the meaning of a question itself partitions the set of indices. Because of the mutual exclusiveness of the cells of a partition, a consequence of G&S's analysis is that, at an index, a question can have at most one true complete (semantic) answer. The idea of treating questions as partitions (of the set of indices or possible states of affairs) seems to have first been proposed by Hamblin (1958); it is also the basis of Higginbotham and May's (1981) analysis, itself based on Levi (1967).

19. In terms of G&S's formal analysis (*cf.* note 18), it is the sense of a question that is embedded under an intensional predicate, *i.e.* there is no free index-variable, while with extensional predicates, as a result of the meaning postulate, the embedding relation is always to the denotation, which contains the free index-variable, just as the matrix clause does.

III

A Nonquantificational Analysis of *Wh*-Phrases, I: Parallels Between *Wh*-Phrases and Indefinites

1 Introduction

In this chapter I will present my analysis, couched within the LHK theory, of a class of sentences which contain complement *wh*-clauses. This is in essence an attempt to carry out the program begun by Nishigauchi (1986; 1990), who analysed certain *wh*-constructions in terms of this theory, but did not develop an explicit semantics nor pursue the consequences of this approach. My general strategy in this chapter is to look for parallels in the quantificational behavior of *wh*-phrases and indefinite NPs.[1] As we saw in chapter I, one of the principal motivations for the LHK treatments of indefinites as logically open sentences is their ability to display quantificational variability; in section 2 of this chapter I will show that *wh*-phrases likewise can be associated with a variety of quantificational forces. I also provide the appropriate restricted quantification representation that accounts for this, in which the *wh*-clause itself serves to restrict the quantifier. In section 3 I adduce independent evidence for this semantic function of *wh*-clauses. In section 4 I propose a general derivation of the restrictive term, based on its containing presuppositions of the nuclear scope, which accounts for a certain asymmetry in the quantifiability of *wh*-phrases. In section 5 I discuss at length the pragmatic variability of many clause-embedding predicates with respect to complement-presupposition.

In this chapter I confine my analysis to sentences in which the *wh*-clause serves to restrict the quantifier; this constitutes the locus of parallel behavior between *wh*-phrases and indefinites, which is the primary motivation for analysing the former within the LHK theory. In chapter V I turn to asymmetries between *wh*-phrases and indefinites.

2 The Quantificational Variability of *Wh*-phrases

In this section I present and discuss the basic data in support of my analysis, and show how they my be accounted for in terms of the LHK theory. As was the case with indefinites, as we saw in chapter I, the empirical motivation for this treatment comes from the variable quantificational force associated with *wh*-phrases under adverbs of quantification.[2] Consider the following sentences:

(25) a. The principal usually finds out which students cheat on the final exam.
      b. Sue mostly remembers which of her birthday presents arrived special delivery.
      c. With few exceptions, Mary knows which students submitted which abstracts to which conferences.
      d. Bill seldom acknowledges which colleagues he gets a good idea from.
      e. John discovered which books were stolen from the library.

The *wh*-phrases here can all be understood as having the quantificational force of the adverb or adverbial phrase in the sentence, as in the following paraphrases:[3]

(26) a. For most students who cheat on the final exam the principal finds out of them that they cheat on the final exam.
      b. For most of her birthday presents that arrived special delivery Sue remembers that they arrived special delivery.
      c. For most triples of a student, an abstract and a conference such that the student submitted the abstract to the conference, Mary knows that the student submitted the abstract to the conference.
      d. For few pairs of a colleague and a good idea such that Bill gets the good idea from the colleague does he acknowledge that he gets the good idea from the colleague.

> e. For all books that were stolen from the library, John discovered that they were stolen from the library.

This quantificational variability of *wh*-phrases under an adverb of quantification parallels that displayed by indefinite NPs, as we saw in chapter I (*cf.* the sentences in (2)). This parallel immediately suggests the possibility of analysing such *wh*-clause-embedding sentences according to the LHK theory.

Apart from the quantificational variability of *wh*-phrases, the paraphrases in (26) reveal several other parallels with indefinites, which further point to a nonquantificational analysis. (25/26.c) shows the binding of more than one *wh*-phrases by a single adverb of quantification, indicating that the "unselectivity" of adverbs of quantification applies to *wh*-phrases (cf. (2.c,d)). Especially striking in this regard is the fact, illustrated by (25/26.d), that a *wh*-phrase and an indefinite can be simultaneously quantified by the same adverb: this is ceteris paribus expected if both phrase types are logically open sentences. Another parallel, exemplified by (26.e), is that, in the absence of an explicit adverb of quantification, the *wh*-phrase is understood to have universal force; I assume, following Lewis, that in such a case there is an implicit default universal quantifier (cf. (2.c)).[4]

Incorporating *wh*-phrases into the LHK theory means, in the first place, that like indefinites in this theory, they will be treated logically as open sentences, expressions that contain an essential free variable. So, for example, the translation for *which students* will be simply student'(x), the same translation as for *a student* and *students* on the LHK theory.[5] Secondly, in view of the theory's use of restricted quantification, we have to determine the restrictive term and the nuclear scope of the quantifier in each case. In section 4 I will argue for a general means of deriving the restrictive term, but for the moment we may let the paraphrases guide us (as we did, in effect, in arriving at the translations for the sentences in (2)): they indicate that it is the *wh*-clause itself that serves to restrict the quantifier, and that the nuclear scope is the entire sentence, except for the adverb. Thus, following the general logical form for restricted quantification in (9), the translations for the sentences in (25) will be as in (27) (again considerably simplified for present purposes):

(27) a. MOST[student'(*x*) & cheat-on-the-final-exam'(*x*)][find-out'(tp,[student'(*x*) & cheat-on-the-final-exam'(*x*)])]

   b. MOST[birthday-present'(*x*) & arrive-special-delivery'(*x*)] [remember'(s,[birthday-present'(*x*) & arrive-special-delivery'(*x*)])]

   c. MOST[student'(*x*) & abstract'(*y*) & conference'(*z*) & submit-to'(*x,y,z*)][know'(m,[student'(*x*) & abstract'(*y*) & conference'(*z*) & submit-to'(*x,y,z*)])]

   d. FEW[colleague'(*x*) & good-idea'(*y*) & get-from'(b,*y,x*)][ac-knowledge'(b,[colleague'(*x*) & good-idea'(*y*) & get-from'(b,*y,x*)])]

   e. ALL[book'(*x*) & be-stolen-from-the-library'(*x*)] [discover'(j,[book'(*x*) & be-stolen-from-the-library'(*x*)])]

It may be noticed that these translations bear a close resemblance to the translations of *wh*-clause-embedding sentences on the Åqvist/Hintikka analysis (*cf.* the translations in (16) of chapter II). In fact, the translations in (27) are a straightforward generalization of this approach. Recall from chapter I that one of the advantages of using restricted quantification is that it captures the full range of quantificational force natural language is capable of, but which cannot be represented by means of truthfunctional connectives in standard first-order logic. The analysis of Åqvist and Hintikka only took into consideration the possibility of universal and existential force for *wh*-phrases, hence could be presented in standard first-order terms. But once we take into account the full quantificational variability of *wh*-phrases, as sentences such as those in (25) force us to do, it is necessary to abandon truthfunctional connectives and move to a more permissive system, such as restrictive quantification.

3 *Wh*-Clauses as Restrictive Terms

The logical translations in (27) for the sentences in (25) were formulated on the basis of the intuitive paraphrases in (26), according to which the translations of the *wh*-clauses themselves serve as the restrictive terms of the quantifiers. In this section I will give independent arguments in support of this logicosemantic function for *wh*-clauses. In particular, I will suggest that an inherent semantic function of *wh*-clauses is to serve as restrictive terms (subject to certain sentence-contextual constraints). Evidence for this comes from parallels with adjunct *if*-clauses, and is further supported by ambiguities in *when*- and *where*-clauses; also, free relatives will be shown to support the restrictive function of *wh*-clauses.

To motivate the claim that a semantic function of *wh*-clauses is to restrict a quantifier, I will take the same tack as I did in arguing for the logical treatment of *wh*-phrases as open sentences, that is, I will look for parallels with other clause types, whose claim to being restrictive terms is more firmly established. The obvious candidate here is *if*-clauses.

3.1 If-*clauses*

We have seen examples of *if*-clauses serving as a restrictive term of an adverb of quantification in examples (2.c,d) of chapter I (and (2.a,b) can be rephrased with an *if*-clause). The idea that *if*-clauses can be restrictive terms, in the sense of restricted quantification theory, is virtually contained in Belnap (1970), who discusses 'if A then B' statements as conditional assertions, *i.e.* assertions that B on condition that A, and goes on to consider such a treatment of restricted universally and existentially quantified statements, *i.e.* 'all A are B' meaning 'consider the set of A: each one is B'. The first explicit claim about this restrictive function appears in the original discussion of adverbs of quantification by Lewis (1975), who, after examining the role of *if*-clauses in the analysis of the quantificational variability of indefinites, says (1975, 11): "I conclude that the *if* of our restrictive *if*-clauses should not be regarded as a sentential connective. It has no meaning apart from the adverb it restricts." Recall that part of the reason for separating the semantics of *if*-clauses from truthfunctional connectives is to account for quantifications involving e.g. MOST and FEW, which have no first-order definition in terms of these connnectives. This claim has subsequently been generalized and defended at length by Kratzer (1978; 1981: in particular, in the analysis of modality, as briefly mentioned in chapter I) and implemented by Heim (1982), as we have seen; Kratzer (1986) is a recent statement of this position.

    In light of this understanding of the role of *if*-clauses, consider
now the following sentences, which correspond to the *wh*-clause-embed-
ding sentences in (25):

(28) a.   The principal usually finds out (about it) if students cheat
           on the final exam.
      b.   Sue usually remembers (it) if a birthday present arrives
           special delivery.
      c.   With few exceptions, Mary knows (about it) if students sub-
           mitted abstracts to conferences.
      d.   Bill seldom acknowledges (it) if he gets a good idea from a
           colleague.
      e.   John always discovers (it) if a book is stolen from the
           library.

These sentences have a number of special properties,[6] which I will
briefly comment on below, but what I want to point out now is that
they each have a reading on which they are synonymous with the
corresponding sentences in (25) (with the exception of (28.b,e), which I
return to directly), that is, the *if*-clause restricts the domain of the
adverb of quantification, and the embedded indefinites are quantified by
the adverb; so that the sentences in (28) may be paraphrased as in (26)
and given the respective logical translations in (27). If a basic semantic
function of *if*-clauses is to restrict a quantifier, and sentences that
embed a *wh*-clause are synonymous with the corresponding sentences
embedding an *if*-clause, then it seems reasonable to conclude that *wh*-
clauses also have such a restrictive function, at least in similar environments.
    The sentences in (28) are ambiguous in ways that those in (25)
are not. One ambiguity has to do with whether the *if*-clause is
understood as a complement of the matrix predicate or as an adjunct to
it (*cf.* Quirk *et al.* (1985, 1053*f*.); *cf.* Jespersen (1961[1928], 42-43) for
speculations on the development of this ambiguity). As adjuncts, the
if-clauses may be preposed, as in the following versions of these sentences:

(29) a.   If a student cheats on the final exam, the principal usually
           finds out (about it).

    b.   If a birthday present arrives special delivery, Sue usually remembers it.

    c.   With few exceptions, if a student submits an abstract to a conference, Mary knows (about it).

    d.   If Bill gets a good idea from a colleague, he seldom acknowledges it.

    e.   If a book is stolen from the library, John always discovers it.

In this form, the sentences have the same pattern as those in (2.c,d). It is as adjuncts that *if*-clauses are able to restrict adverbs of quantification; apparently they are not able to do so as complement clauses (I return to this issue in appendix C)[7]. Henceforth, unless otherwise noted, when I cite a sentence with an ambiguous *if*-clause, I mean it to be taken as an adjunct. Note that on the reading under consideration the correlative *it*, which with some verbs may be omitted, is anaphoric to the *if*-clause, so is realized in the logical representation as the same open sentence that translates the *if*-clause. The presence of the correlative pronoun in the sentences in (28) forces the *if*-clause to be interpreted as an adjunct, thought if the correlative is omitted, the adjunct reading still seems to be possible in many cases. (There is an additional ambiguity with some of these sentences, where *it* is not correlative but anaphoric to the indefinite; this is then a standard case of donkey anaphora.)

    The lack of synonymy between (28.b,e) and (25.b,e) is due the difference in aspect: the latter are episodic, while the former are habitual or generic. It seems that *if*-clauses are not able to restrict adverbs of quantification if the aspect of the *if*-clause is episodic, as in the following sentences:

(30)   a.   If a birthday present arrived special delivery, Sue (*usually) remembered it.

          b.   If books were stolen from the library, John (*always) discovered it.

With the adverbs of quantification, the sentences are ungrammatical (these adverbs also require habitual or generic aspect). Without the adverbs, the sentences are grammatical, but have a particular, nonquantificational, interpretation. Specifically, they are epistemic conditionals. That is, the sentences are reporting what must be the case, in view of what we know. The role of the *if*-clause here is to restrict the epistemic modal operator (*cf.* Kratzer (1981)); the sentences in (30) are thus synonymous with the following (where *must* is understood epistemically, not deontically):

(31) a. If a birthday present arrived special delivery, Sue must have remembered it.
      b. If books were stolen from the library, John must have discovered it.

Kratzer (1989) observes that epistemic modals appear unable to bind variables (unlike some other modals, *e.g.* those that have a more lawlike interpretation); thus the indefinites in (30) and (31) are not quantified by the modal. If they were, they would have universal force; instead, they are understood existentially, which on the LHK theory is attributed to the effect of existential closure, *i.e.* they are assigned values by g'' in the truth definition in (10) in chapter 1.[8]

3.2 When- *and* Where-*clauses*

In addition to *if*-clauses, Lewis (1975) also observed that *when-*, *where-*, and participial clauses also may function as restrictive terms, (on *when*-clauses, *cf.* Farkas and Sugioka (1983), Partee (1984), and Declerck (1988); on participial clauses, and free adjuncts generally, *cf.* Stump (1985)). Lewis gives the following examples for *when* and *where* (1975(44,46)):

(32) a. When m and n are positive integers, the power m^n can always be computed by succesive multiplications.
      b. The power m^n, where m and n are positive integers, can always be computed by succesive multiplications.

When and *where* are also, of course, *wh*-words, which means, on my analysis, that their logical translations should contain an essential free variable, and they should display quantificational variability; the following sentences indicate that this is correct:

(33) a. Mary mostly knows when they feed Xing-Xing the panda at the zoo.

     b. John mostly knows where they sell Poccino espresso machines.

In these sentences *when* and *where* are acting semantically as sortals over temporal and spatial locations, respectively. In addition, the whole *when-* and *where*-clause in each case is clearly restricting the quantifier: the sentences are about most times they feed Xing-Xing the panda at the zoo and most places they sell Poccino espresso machines. This further supports the claim that *wh*-clauses, generally, can be restrictive terms. The sentences in (33) receive the following (simplified) translations in the LHK theory (where TIME and PLACE are to be taken, for simplicity, as the appropriate sortal predicates):

(34) a. MOST[TIME(x) & they-feed-Xing-Xing-the-panda'(x)] [know'(m,[TIME(x) & they-feed-Xing-Xing-the-panda'(x)])]

     b. MOST[PLACE(x) & they-sell-Poccino-espresso-machines'(x)][know'(j,[PLACE(x) & they-sell-Poccino-espresso-machines'(x)])]

Another expected consequence is that when these clauses contain an indefinite NP, an ambiguity arises, as the following sentence illustrates:

(35) The principal usually finds out when a student cheats on the final exam.

This may have the same reading as (29.a) (and (25.a)), represented by the translation in (27.a), but in addition, it may have a reading in which pairs of a student and a time at which the student cheats are quantified over; it even seems possible that just the *wh*-phrase, not the indefinite, may be quantified, meaning that the principal finds out most times at which there are students who cheat. It is on the last two readings that *when* is translated as an open sentence, *i.e.* a sortal predicate over temporal intervals, as in (33.a). The two (or three) readings are usually distinguishable in speech by intonation: if there is no pause prior to the *when*-clause and *when* is accented, the quantification is over (at least) occasions; if there is a pause and *when* is deaccented, the quantification is over students (*cf.* also Quirk *et al.* (1985)). On the reading where *when* is a sortal over temporal intervals, the *when*-clause is a syntactic complement of the matrix predicate; whereas, when the quantification is over students (only), the *when*-clause is syntactically an adjunct, that is, it is essentially semantically the same as the adjunct *if*-clauses discussed in the previous subsection. The difference in intonation supports this distinction, which is a standard grammatical one (*cf.* Quirk *et al.*). Moreover, as an adjunct, the *when*-clause, like an adjunct *if*-clause, may be preposed:

(36)   When a student cheats on the final exam, the principal usually finds out.

In this sentence, as expected, the quantificational reading only involves students, *i.e.*, the logical translation is that in (27.a). On the sortal reading of *when*, the clause may not be preposed: (36) cannot mean that most times at which a student cheats on the final exam are such that the principal finds out that a student cheats at that time. (As a temporal sortal, *when* is just a normal *wh*-word, and undergoes *wh*-movement, whereas as a nonsortal, it basically serves just to mark a restrictive term, like *if* (perhaps with some additional temporal element, but not one that can itself be quantified); I will argue in chapter V that the quantificational behavior of *wh*-phrases is largely a consequence of the fact that they undergo *wh*-movement.)

3.3 Free Relatives

Free relatives are semantically clausal, like *wh*-complement clauses (indirect questions), but syntactically they have the distribution of NPs (for the most part) (their internal syntactic composition is a matter of long-standing controversy, though the recent concensus favors the internal syntax of an ordinary *wh*-clause, a position I accept).[9] Typical examples are the following:

(37)   a.   Mary likes who she meets.
        b.   John eats what he grows in his vegetable garden.
        c.   What Sue paints is beautiful.

Now, the *wh*-phrase in a free relative can have variable quantificational force, as the following sentence illustrate:[10]

(38) a. Mary seldom likes who she meets.
      b. John mostly eats what he grows in his vegetable garden.
      c. What Sue paints is often beautiful.

These sentences have the following respective paraphrases:

(39) a. Few people Mary meets are such that she likes them.
      b. Most things John grows in his vegetable garden (i.e. most vegetables John grows) are such that he eats them.
      c. Many things Sue paints (i.e. many paintings by Sue), are beautiful.

As these paraphrases indicate, the *wh*-clause—*i.e.* the entire free relative—is restricting the quantifier, just as with indirect questions. That this is the case is also supported by the fact that correponding to the sentences in (38) are synonymous sentences with *if*- or *when*-clauses containing an indefinite:

(40) a. If Mary meets someone, she seldom likes him.
      b. When John grows vegetables in his garden, he mostly eats them.
      c. When Sue makes a painting, it is often beautiful.

A difference between free relatives and indirect questions, however, is that, whereas the latter appear in both the restrictive term and the nuclear scope, the former appear only in the restrictive term, as indicated by the paraphrases and the corresponding *if*- and *when*-clauses (note there is no correlative pronoun anaphoric to the free relative clause); thus, the translations of the sentences in (38) are as follows:[11]

(41) a. FEW[PERSON(x) & meet'(m,x)][like'(m,x)]
      b. MOST[vegetable'(x) & grow-in-garden'(j,x)][eat'(j,x)]
      c. MANY[painting'(x) & paint'(s,x)][beautiful'(x)]

I will return, in chapter V, section 3.3, after I have developed my analysis more fully, to a possible account of this difference between free relatives and indirect questions. Notwithstanding this difference, however, the interpretation of free relatives provides further justification, also supported by the parallel *if-* and *when*-clauses, for the claim that *wh*-clauses in general are restrictive terms.

3.4 Summary

I have argued that a semantic function of *wh*-clauses is to serve as (part of) the restrictive term of a quantifier; support for this conclusion comes from parallels with (adjunct) *if*-clauses, which have been independently argued to have such a restrictive function, as well as ambiguities with *when-* and *where*-clauses, and the behavior of free relatives. The question now arises, do *wh*-clauses always have this restrictive function, or are there environments where they are prevented from restricting a quantifier, and if so, what then is their semantic role? I will begin to address these questions in the next section.

4 Deriving the Restrictive Term: Presupposition

I will argue that the ability of an embedded *wh*-clause to serve as the restrictive term of a quantifier is directly connected to a certain relation it bears to the matrix clause it is embedded in, and that, furthermore, the possibility of being in this relation is one of the properties that distinguishes between two logicosemantically separate types of *wh*-clauses. By making such a distinction between *wh*-clauses, the analysis will also avoid a problem inherent in the formulation given to this point. I noted at the end of section 2 above that my analysis is in essence a generalization of the Åqvist/Hintikka approach. But we saw in chapter II, section 3, that this approach has difficulty accounting for sentences with predicates that embed *wh*-clauses but do not embed *that*-clauses, and it would seem that my analysis should have the same difficulty. It is to avoid this difficulty that I introduce a distinction between *wh*-clause types. I show that there is independent motivation for such a distinction, accounting for facts apparently unrelated to the inability of embedding a *that*-clause but intimately connected with the possibility of the *wh*-clause to serve as a restrictive term (I return to the formal implementation of the proposed bipartition of *wh*-clauses in chapter V). The independent motivation in fact points to a general process involved in the derivation of the restrictive term of a quantified sentence, a process that in itself has nothing to do with the analysis of *wh*-constructions.

4.1 A Quantificational Asymmetry

In light of the main conclusion of section 3, that *wh*-clauses can restrict an adverb of quantification, consider the following sentences, which differ from the corresponding sentences in (25) superficially only in the choice of matrix predicate:

(42) a. The principal usually wonders which students cheat on the final exam.

      b. Sue mostly asked which of her birthday presents arrived special delivery.

      c. With few exceptions, Mary is interested in which students submitted which abstracts to which conferences.

      d. Bill seldom thinks about which colleagues he gets a good idea from.

      e. John investigated which books were stolen from the library.

These sentences, unlike the sentences in (25), do not have a reading on which the *wh*-clause restricts the adverb of quantification. Now, to be sure, I cannot give paraphrases of these sentences like those I have given in (26) for the sentences in (25), simply because the matrix predicates of the sentences in (42) do not take a *that*-clause. But that might be beside the point, because the logical translations on my analysis do not in any case contain a *that*-clause; in other words, the question is (in addition to the question of what the translations and interpretations in fact are), why doesn't *e.g.* (42.a) have the following translation:

(43) $MOST[student'(x)$ & $cheat\text{-}on\text{-}the\text{-}final\text{-}exam'(x)]$
    $[wonder'(tp,[student'(x) \& cheat\text{-}on\text{-}the\text{-}final\text{-}exam'(x)])]$

This would be true, according to the definition in (10) from chapter I, if and only if for most students x such that x cheated on the final exam, the principal stands in the wondering relation to the proposition that x is a student and x cheated on the final exam. But this is simply not what (42.a) means. To evaluate the truth of that sentence we do not need to consider the number of students (if any) who did well on the exam. What, then, are the truth conditions of that sentence?

I don't want to go into my formal analysis of the meanings of the sentences in (42) just yet (that will be done in chapter V), but in order for it to be clear that they don't involve the *wh*-clause restricting the adverb, I will spell out intuitively what I think they mean. For (42.a), for instance, we need only ascertain that the principal has before her appropriate possible values for x in 'x is a student and x cheated on the final exam' and is in the wondering relation to the set of propositions determined by supplying these values to x—whether or not they are true in the actual situation. In other words, we have to determine that the principal is in the wondering relation to the question "Which students did well on the exam?" (*cf.* Hamblin's semantics for questions, chapter II, section 4.1.1). The adverb *usually* is not functioning as an adverb of quantification, *i.e.* as a quantifier over students who do well on the exam (or perhaps over situations containing such students). Rather, it is functioning as a frequency quantifier over temporals intervals of the principal's wondering, so that a paraphrase might be: "For most times that the principal wonders, she wonders which students cheat on the final exam." (Possibly there is a reading where the adverb quantifies over final exam situations, so that the paraphrase would be: "For most final exams, the principal wonders which students cheat on them." *Cf.* chapter IV, section 2.)

Although, as I noted, unlike the matrix predicates in (25) those in (42) only embed *wh*-clauses, not also *that*-clauses, this difference appears not to be decisive; the following sentences parallel those in (42) in that the *wh*-clauses are also not understood to restrict the adverbs (on salient readings—I return to this below), although the matrix predicates here also embed *that*-clauses:

(44)   a.   The principal usually speculates which students cheat on the final exam.

     b.   Sue mostly persuaded herself which of her birthday presents arrived special delivery.

     c.   With few exceptions, Mary imagined which students submitted which abstracts to which conferences.

    d.   Bill seldom decides which colleagues he gets a good idea from.

    e.   John contemplated which books were stolen from the library.

4.2 Factivity and Presupposition

So neither the sentences in (42) nor those in (44) have readings on which the adverb is restricted by the *wh*-clause as a whole. As I noted, the only superficial difference between these sentences and those in (25), in which the *wh*-clause does restrict the adverb, is in the respective matrix predicates. There is in fact a well-known difference between the matrix predicates in (25) (*find out, remember, acknowledge, know, discover*) on one hand, and those in (42) and (44) (*wonder, ask, be interested in, think about, investigate* and *speculate, persuade oneself, imagine, decide, contemplate*) on the other: the former are typical examples of so-called factive predicates, while the latter are instances of nonfactive predicates. This terminology was used by Kiparsky and Kiparsky (1971[1970]) to classify predicates according to a number of syntactic and semantic criteria. The syntactic features are not that relevant here, but Kiparsky and Kiparsky's semantic diagnostic is crucial: they say that in the utterance of a sentence whose matrix predicate is factive "[t]he speaker presupposes that the embedded clause expresses a true proposition," while no such presupposition is associated with nonfactive predicates (1971, 348).[12] To illustrate, the verbs *regret* and *believe* are typical factive and nonfactive predicates, respectively. Thus, it is presupposed that the complement in (45.a) expresses a true proposition, i.e. that Mary left, while there is no such presupposition regarding the complement in (45.b):

(45)   a.   John regrets that Mary left.
        b.   John believes that Mary left.

I will argue that we can use the difference between factive and nonfactive predicates to correctly distinguish between the sentences in (25) and those in (42) and (44) by suitably adapting Kiparsky and Kiparsky's characterization and by making a hypothesis. The hypothesis is the following: in the logical representation of a quantified sentence (as analyzed in terms of restricted quantification), the presuppositions of the nuclear scope become part of the restrictive term.[13],[14] The adaptation is needed in view of the reference to the presuppositions of the nuclear scope. Since this piece of logical representation is an open sentence, it does not denote a proposition, has no truthvalue in and of itself. The adaptation I propose is to separate the notions of presupposition and truth, and simply to define presuppositions essentially syntactically, as linguistic representations that bear a certain relation to some other linguistic representation. (Nevertheless, this syntactic relation is firmly grounded in the lexical semantics of the predicates involved. If this characterization of presupposition is felt to be an obfuscation, then it might be better simply to call it the presuppositional contribution of the nuclear scope; but I will adhere to the term presupposition.) I will characterize this relation in the case of factivity by saying that factive predicates presuppose their complements and nonfactive predicates do not presuppose their complements.[15] Let me illustrate.

The matrix predicate in (45.a) is factive, so it presupposes its complement, which is the syntactic structure [that Mary left]; this happens to be a proposition-denoting expression. We can give the logical representation of (45.a) as the following:

(46)   [left'(m)] & [regret'(j,[left'(m)])]

This will be true if and only if both conjuncts are true, and this captures Kiparsky and Kiparsky's idea that the factive presupposes the truth of its complement. Now consider (25.a), repeated here:

(25)   a.   The principal usually finds out which students cheat on the final exam.

The nuclear scope of this quantified sentence is the following:

(47)   [find-out'(tp,[student'(x) & cheat-on-the-final-exam'(x)])]

Again, the matrix predicate here is factive so presupposes its complement. According to the above hypothesis, this becomes part of the restrictive term. Adding the quantifier, the resulting structure is just the representation (27.a), repeated here:

(27) a.   MOST[student'(x) & cheat-on-the-final-exam'(x)][find-
out'(tp,[student'(x) & cheat-on-the-final-exam'(x)])]

This structure yields the intuitively correct truthconditions for (25.a),
as we have seen.

It is important, however, not to identify the presupposition of
(47) as a presupposition of (25.a). For one thing, the former is a logical representation and the latter is a sentence. But the crucial point is
that in becoming part of the restrictive term, the presupposition of the
nuclear scope remains inside the quantified structure, *i.e.* it is not
independent of it, as is, for example, the presupposition in the nonquantificational (45.a). In consequence of this, it may well not survive
as a presupposition of the sentence as a whole. The point is especially
clear if we consider the *if*-clause variant (29.a) of (25.a), repeated here:

(29) a.   If a student cheats on the final exam, the principal usually
finds out (about it).

Here too, the presupposition of the nuclear scope is [student'(x) &
cheat-on-the-final-exam'(x)], which is the translation of the *if*-clause,
which, as we have seen, is a canonical restrictive term. However, it is
well-known that in conditional sentences in which the antecedent (*if*-
clause) contains the presuppositions of the consequent, these do not
survive as presuppositions of the whole sentence (*cf.* Karttunen (1973),
Gazdar (1979), Levinson (1983), Soames (1989), among others). Nevertheless, we still can say that the presuppositions of the nuclear scope
are part of the restrictive term.[16]

We see, then, how this hypothesis accounts for the interpretations of the sentences in (25), by in effect deriving the respective
translations in (27): in each the nuclear scope consists of the translation of the whole sentence minus that of the adverb of quantification;
since the matrix predicate is factive, it presupposes its complement, the
wh-clause, in the sense explained above, which by hypothesis becomes
part of the restrictive term; and this yields the translation we have seen
to be necessary for the correct intepretation of these sentences. On the
other hand, if we try to derive similar translations for the sentences in
(42) and (44) by applying this hypothesis, we will not succeed, because
the matrix predicates there are nonfactive, they do not presuppose their
complement, which hence cannot by this means become part of the

restrictive term; assuming there is no other way for the *wh*-clause to become part of the restrictive term, such translations are not derivable, accounting for the lack of the associated interpretation for these sentences.

4.3 Presupposition Accommodation

It will be convenient to have a term to refer to the process by which the restrictive term incorporates the presuppositions of the nuclear scope. In fact this process bears some resemblance to a well-known principle of conversational dynamics, which Lewis (1979) called presupposition accommodation. This is a general regulatory process for maintaining conversational felicity, whose basic idea is the following (this goes back to Stalnaker (1973), *cf.* Soames (1989)). Conversations take place in contexts containing certain information which the participants in the conversation take for granted, assume to be the case: this is the conversational background. Sometimes one of the participants makes an utterance that presupposes information that is not in the conversational background, say because it is not known to (or at least taken for granted by) the other participants. In this case what typically happens is that the information in question is automatically admitted into the conversational background, which is in effect retroactively readjusted to reflect the presence of the new information, so that the utterance that made the presupposition is interpretable. For example, if Mary tells Bill, who knows nothing about her musical interests, "I'm taking piano lessons again," then Bill will immediately accommodate the presupposition that Mary used to take piano lessons, thus correctly understanding the utterance. In the case of quantified sentences such as those in (25), which also make presuppositions, a similar process of accommodation takes place, but with the specific effect on the logical representation that the presupposition becomes part of the restrictive term. I will thus say that the presuppositions of the nuclear scope are accommodated into the restricted term.[17]

In fact, that presupposition accommodation has this effect on quantified sentence has been noted on numerous occasions.[18] The following example adapted from Schubert and Pelletier (1989) clearly shows the effect of accommodation in a quantified sentence:

(48)   A cat always lands on its feet.

Schubert and Pelletier observe (p.194) that this sentence "is not evaluated as if it said that at all or most times cats are landing on their feet, but rather a certain class of 'cases' or 'situations' is set up—such as all those cases where cats drop to the ground—and the sentence is evaluated with respect to those cases." Indeed, it can be regarded as a lexical presupposition of the verb *land* that the thing that lands (if any) was previously in the air, and our knowledge of cats tells us that they cannot fly, so dropping to the ground is a natural situation to qualify as the restrictive term of the quantifier in the logical representation of (48); this sentence would thus have the following logical translation on the LHK analysis:[19]

(49)   ALL [cat'(x) & drop-to-the-ground'(x)][land-on-its-feet'(x)]

Note, moreover, that this translation is what the LHK theory would assign to the following sentence too:

(50)   If/When a cat drops to the ground, it always lands on its feet.

As we have seen in section 3 above, (adjunct) *if-* and *when*-clauses are canonical restrictive terms, so the synonymy between (48) and (50) further supports the accommodation of the presupposition of the nuclear scope into the restrictive term as a general process. (It must of course be borne in mind that, as noted above, this presupposition does not in general survive as a presupposition of the sentence as a whole.) Further examples involving presupposition accommodation into the restrictive term are the following sentences, with corresponding *if/when*-clause paraphrases:

(51)   a.   A go master usually beats a novice.
       b.   When a go master plays a novice, he usually beats him.
(52)   a.   A slob seldom uses a napkin.
       b.   When a slob eats, he seldom uses a napkin.
(53)   a.   An honest citizen usually pays a parking ticket.
       b.   If/When an honest citizen gets a parking ticket, he usually
            pays it.
(54)   a.   A graduate student often wakes up after noon.

      b.   When a graduate student has been sleeping, he often wakes up after noon.

(55) a.   John usually finishes reading an article by Chomsky.
      b.   If/When John has been reading an article by Chomsky, he usually finishes reading it.

(56) a.   John usually manages to see a film by Fellini.
      b.   If John tries to see a film by Fellini, he usually manages to see it.

(57) a.   John usually sees a film by Fellini a second time.
      b.   If John sees a film by Fellini once, he usually sees it a second time.

(58) a.   John usually regrets missing a lecture.
      b.   If/When John misses a lecture, he usually regrets missing it.

The examples in (51)-(54) are further cases of specific lexical presuppositions. The other examples are instances of more general presupposition triggers, that is, types of constructions that induce presuppositions (see *e.g.* Levinson (1983, 181*ff.*) and Soames (1989, 571*f.*) for longer lists and discussion of presupposition triggers). (55) exemplifies the change of state trigger ((54) also involves a change of state, but it is inherent in the meaning of *wake up*, rather than induced by a separate item, such as *finish*); (56) is an implicative construction (Karttunen (1971)); (57) illustrates the iterative trigger. (58) is another example of presupposition induced by factivity, here involving a nonfinite complement.

      In short, there is considerable evidence to support the hypothesis that the presuppositions of the nuclear scope of a quantifier are accommodated into its restrictive term. And we have seen that this hypothesis accounts for the quantificational asymmetry we observed between the sentences in (25) and those in (42) and (44) by effectively deriving the translations that yield the intuitively correct interpretations of the former sentences, while not sanctioning similar derivations for the latter sentences. There being no other way for the translations of the complement to become part of the restrictive term of the quantifier in these sentences, the corresponding interpretation is not generated by the analysis, again according with our intuitions. While the simplicity of this account is quite appealing, as is often the case in empirical research, there are data that point to a more intricate picture; I discuss these complications in the next section.

5 The Presuppositional Vagueness of Clause-embedding Predicates

5.1 Unexpected Cases of Quantifiability

My derivation of the restrictive term of quantified sentences by presupposition accommodation from the nuclear scope was predicated on the observation that the matrix predicates of the sentences in (25) are factive while those of the sentences in (42) and (44) are nonfactive: given the well-known claim that factive predicates presuppose their complement while nonfactive predicates do not, the hypothesis of presupposition accommodation accounts for the difference in interpretation between the two groups of sentences. In view of such desirable consequences of this factivity-based explanation, it is unexpected to encounter sentences such as the following:

(59) The teacher usually tells the principal which students cheat on the final exam.

This sentence has an interpretation paraphrasable as: for most students who cheat on the final exam, the teacher tells the principal that they cheat on the final exam. In other words, it has the following logical translation:

(60) MOST[student'(x) & cheat-on-the-final-exam'(x)][tell'(tt,tp, [student'(x) & cheat-on-the-final-exam'(x)])]

And yet, *tell* is generally taken to be a nonfactive predicate; for example, in the following sentence it is not presupposed that the complement is true:

(61) The teacher told the principal that John cheated on the final exam.

In fact, I already noted in chapter II a similar observation about the presuppositional status of *wh*-clauses under apparently nonfactive verbs, due to Baker (1968), which prompted Karttunen's analysis according to which questions denote the set of their true answers (*cf.* section 4.1.2). The sentences in (62) are additional cases in point.

(62)   a.   Sue mostly guessed which of her birthday presents arrived special delivery.
       b.   With few exceptions, Mary decided which students submitted which abstracts to which conferences.
       c.   Bill seldom indicates which colleagues he gets a good idea from.
       d.   John contemplated which books were stolen from the library.

This factive behavior of these apparently nonfactive verbs seems to call into question my presupposition-based approach to deriving the restrictive term.

Notwithstanding this seeming difficulty, I would like to maintain the basic idea that the logical translation of a quantified sentence with an embedded *wh*-clause is derived by presupposition accommodation from the nuclear scope to the restrictive term. I will try to show that with many clause-embedding predicates it is not fixed once and for all in their lexical meaning that they do or do not presuppose their complement, that is, that many predicates are not simply either factive or nonfactive. Rather, sometimes a given predicate may be understood factively, as presupposing its complement, but in another context it may be understood nonfactively. Indeed, this should not be surprising, given the pragmatic basis of presupposition.

5.2   On the Pragmatic Variability of Factivity

It will be helpful to begin with to have an inventory of the kinds of predicates that embed *wh*-clauses. Baker (1968) proposed a fourfold classification, consisting of *know*-predicates, *decide*-predicates, *matter*-predicates, and *depend*-predicates. Karttunen (1977), largely by subdividing the first class, produced the following list:

(63) a. retaining knowledge: *know, be aware, recall, remember, forget*
  b. acquiring knowledge: *learn, notice, find out, discover*
  c. communication: *tell, show, indicate, inform, disclose*
  d. decision: *decide, determine, specify, agree on, control*
  e. conjecture: *guess, predict, bet on, estimate*
  f. opinion: *be certain about, have an idea about, be convinced of*
  g. inquisitive: *ask, wonder, investigate, be interested in*
  h. relevance: *matter, be relevant, be important, care, be significant*
  i. dependency: *depend on, be related to, have an influence on, be a function of, make a difference to*

There are a number of other groups of *wh*-clause-embedding predicates that call for further subdivisions of this classification or should be listed as separate classes:

(63) j. realization: *realize, understand, perceive, grasp*
  k. sensation: *sense, see, discern, hear, feel*
  l. imagining: *imagine, visualize, picture (to oneself), envision, envisage*
  m. contemplation: *contemplate, consider, reflect upon, ponder, think about*
  n. argumentation: *argue, dispute, debate (about), reason (about)*
  o. evaluation: *evaluate, assess, judge, deduce, infer, conclude, derive*
  p. explanation: *explain, account for*
  q. verification: *verify, prove, confirm, establish, ascertain*
  r. justification: *justify, rationalize, excuse, apologize (for)*
  s. (in)attention: *pay attention to, disregard, note, bear in mind, overlook*
  t. anticipation: *anticipate, wait and see[20], be excited (about)*
  u. surprise: *be surprised/amazed/astonished (at)*
  v. (dis)pleasure: *be (dis)pleased/(un)happy/delighted (about/at/with)*

This list can certainly be extended, although many of the entries could be subsumed under one or another of the headings in Karttunen's classi-

fication (just as his groups (63.a,b,c,e,f,g) were classified by Baker as
know-predicates). The verbs of realization are clearly knowledge verbs,
also the verbs of sensation (in one sense); the verbs of contemplation
could be grouped with the inquisitive verbs (*wonder* indeed seems more
contemplative than inquisitive); the evaluative verbs might go with the
verbs of decision or conjecture, perhaps too the verbs of argumentation
(or maybe they are communicative); verbs of explanation are clearly
also communicative, as are the verbs of justification, and both groups
could probably be treated as involving retaining knowledge; the verbs
of verification certainly may be communicative but seem also to be
able to involve acquiring knowledge, as do the verbs of surprise; and so
on. But my interest here is not so much in finding an optimal group-
ing of *wh*-clause-embedding predicates as in investigating how they
pattern with respect to factivity.

Among the categories in Karttunen's list, the verbs of knowledge and relevance are by and large factive; all the other groups are
generally taken to be nonfactive (with the verbs of dependency it may
not be so clear). Among the groups extending Karttunen's list, the
nonfactive ones are the verbs of imagining, contemplation, argumentation, evaluation, and anticipation; the rest appear to be factive. Notwithstanding these rough generalizations, I want to suggest that, upon
closer examination of the behavior of some of these groups, and some
of the individual predicates, hard and fast classification may not be
appropriate.

I should at this point also acknowledge that in their original
discussion, Kiparsky and Kiparsky recognized not just the bipartition
factive/nonfactive, but also a third group, which they called indifferent
with respect to factivity (they meant this to apply to their syntactic
criteria, as well as to the presuppositional status of the complement).
Among the predicates they cite as indifferent, which also embed *wh*-
clauses, are *anticipate, acknowledge*[21], *report, remember, emphasize,
announce, deduce*. These include verbs of knowledge, communication,
evaluation, and anticipation. In fact, the verbs of communication,
broadly taken, are a quite unhomogeneous class. They include a great
many verbs, many of which, e.g. the verbs of explanation, verification,
and justification, certainly seem to count as factive; these should
include *disclose* and probably *show* (in the sense of *prove*). Others,
such as *tell*, as I noted above, are usually considered to be nonfactive.

However, it has also been observed that many verbs which are usually taken to be nonfactive or indifferent with respect to factivity, when negated tend to be understood as presupposing their complement, as in the following sentence (from Gazdar (1979, 117)):

(64) The repairman didn't tell me that my camera was suitable for color too.

Here are some more examples:

(65) a. Mary didn't guess that Bill was over thirty.
b. John didn't envisage that Sue was a closet iguana-lover.
c. George didn't anticipate that Jane was a vegetarian.
Helen forgot to announce that the meeting was cancelled.

Conversely, it has also been pointed out that under negation factive verbs sometimes fail to presuppose their complements, as in the following examples:

(66) a. I don't know that Bill is over thirty.
b. John didn't discover that there is a largest prime number (because in fact there isn't).
c. Sue isn't unhappy that she missed the concert, because in fact it was cancelled.

Also, in negative modal contexts, the same sort of switch sometimes appears:

(67) a. George couldn't have anticipated that Jane was a vegetarian.
b. Sue couldn't be unhappy that she missed the concert, because in fact it was cancelled.

These data suggest that factivity, *i.e.* presupposition of the complement, is often not simply a lexically fixed property of a predicate but rather context-dependent.

With many predicates we can notice an ambiguity of meaning that precisely correlates with whether their complement is presupposed or not. When it is presupposed, it is taken to be true (at least within the scope of higher operators), and this is reflected in the meaning of

the predicate. Some examples: *guess* means either find out by guess-
ing, *i.e.* guess correctly (complement presupposed), or just offer an
opinion, i.e. take a guess (complement not presupposed)[22]; presuppositional *anticipate* means guess correctly and plan accordingly, nonpresuppositional *anticipate* means look forward to; presuppositional *decide*
means cause to be realized through the power of decision, nonpre-
suppositionally it means make up your mind, *i.e.* reach a decision. A
similar difference is reflected in the possibility with some predicates of
taking complex NP complements, where the NP is either *the fact*, if
the complement clause is presupposed, or *the question*, if it is not:

(68)   a.   The principal contemplated the fact that Bill cheated.
       b.   The principal contemplated the question whether Bill
            cheated.
(69)   a.   John is interested in the fact that Sue likes iguanas.
       b.   John is interested in the question whether Sue likes iguanas.

All of these verbs can participate in quantificational sentences when
taking a *wh*-complement, with the latter restricting an adverb of quantification. I illustrated this in (61) and (62) above for *tell, guess, decide,
indicate,* and *contemplate*; several of the sentences in (42) and (44) can
also be understood this way—note, in particular, that (62.d), which
illustrates this for the last verb, is the same sentence as (44.e), which I
claimed doesn't have this reading: the distinction is just that in the
latter case it is contemplation of the question whether while in the
former it is contemplation of the fact that. In some cases the situation
described by the sentences favors the presuppositional over the nonpre-
suppostional reading or vice versa: *cf.* (62.b) and (44.d), where in the
former we might imagine Mary to be a professor or referee, while to
get the presuppositional reading in the latter we'd have to take Bill to
wield control over his colleagues' giving examples.

      This ambiguity between presuppositional and nonpresupposi-
tional readings of certain predicates may also shed light on the
following sentences, which have the same matrix predicates as those in
(42) but instead of embedding *wh*-clauses have adjunct *if*-clauses:

(70)   a.   If a student cheats on the final exam, the principal usually
            wonders about it.

    b.   If a birthday present of hers arrives special delivery, Sue seldom asks about it.

    c.   With few exceptions, if a student submits an abstract to a conference, Mary is interested (in it).

    d.   If Bill gets a good idea from a colleague, he seldom thinks about it.

    e.   If a book is stolen from the library, John investigates it.

In these sentences, the *if*-clause both restricts the adverb of quantification and is understood as part of the nuclear scope as well. That is, (70.a), for example, has the following logical translation (*cf.* (43) above):

(71)   MOST[student'(x) & cheat-on-the-final-exam'(x)][wonder-about'(tp,[student'(x) & cheat-on-the-final-exam'(x)])]

Notice, moreover, that in each of these sentences the correlative *it*, which is anaphoric to the *if*-clause, could be meaning-preservingly replaced by *that fact* but not by *that question*, although all the matrix predicates here can take either of these complex NPs. (There is also the donkey reading for several of these sentences, as was noted for some of the sentences in (29) in section 3.1 above, where *it* is anaphoric not to the whole *if*-clause but just to the indefinite NP in it.) This seems to me to support the effect of the presuppositional/nonpresuppositional ambiguity I have been discussing, and indirectly the derivation of the restrictive term through presupposition accommodation. To be sure, the *if*-clauses are restrictive terms independent of accommodation, but the fact that they can also be understood as part of the nuclear scope can be seen as evidence for the presuppositional reading of the matrix predicates.

    This raises a question, however, which I do not have a good answer to. Namely, why can't all *wh*-clause-embedding predicates be understood presuppositionally, and thus have their complements accommodated into the restrictive term? For indeed, I think that (42.a,b), for example, cannot be understood in the way that (70.a,b) can. It may be relevant that the respective matrix predicates in these pairs of sentence do seem to have slightly different meanings, perhaps signalled by the necessity to use a preposition with the latter pair: while in (42.a,b) the verbs are interrogative about the content of their *wh*-complements, which are correspondingly understood simply to provide a set of possibilities, in (70.a,b) the interrogation does not seem to be about the content of the *if*-clauses, which is taken for granted (because presupposed), but rather about some aspect of this content, *e.g.* why this is the fact. A similar distinction seems to obtain with the verbs *discuss, argue about*, and *speculate about*: when embedding a *wh*-clause, these too do not have a presuppositional reading, but with an *if*-adjunct, they can have such an understanding, with a similar difference as with *wonder* and *ask*, indicated by the ability to take the complex NP *the fact*:

(72) a. The principal usually discusses/argues/speculates about which students cheat on the final exam.
       b. If a student cheat on the final exam, the principal usually discusses/argues/speculates about it/that fact.

It appears, then, that, if a suitable restrictive term is independently available, as is the case with *if*-clauses, then unambiguously nonfactive predicates can have a kind of factive reading. This, however, stills leaves unexplained why, when these predicates embed *wh*-clauses, presupposition accommodation appears not to be possible. Acknowledging that this signals a gap in my account, I will now consider two other attempts to explain the variable behavior of *wh*-clause-embedding predicates, in terms of the semantics either of the predicates or of the *wh*-clauses; I will show that these alternatives are explanatorily unsatisfactory.

5.3 Two Semantic Alternatives

5.3.1 G&S: Intensional and Extensional Predicates

Recall (chapter II, section 4.2 and note 18) that G&S treat embedded *wh*-clauses as relations between indices, whose evaluation is independent of the index at which the matrix clause is evaluated. This has the consequence that the proposition their account assigns to the embedded clause may not be true at the matrix index. In effect, G&S treat all *wh*-clause-embedding predicates as nonfactive. In order to account for the factive interpretation with verbs such as *know* they introduce a meaning postulate which extensionalizes the relation between the matrix predicate and the embedded clause, that is, makes the latter's index of evaluation the same as that of the matrix clause, thus tying the truth of the two together.

Despite my above characterization, one of the things that G&S claim about this division of predicates as intensional or extensional is that it is independent of the factive/nonfactive distinction. As evidence, they cite the behavior of *tell*, which they take to be nonfactive, but which is extensional in that its complement is evaluated at the same index as it is. But this is what would be the case if *tell* were factive, since *know* behaves this way; as we have seen, there do indeed appear to be circumstances where *tell* behave like a factive predicate, even when its complement is not a *wh*-clause (*cf.* (64)). And we have seen that this kind of factivity-switch happens with a great many predicates. One of these, *guess*, G&S classify as intensional. This raises the question for their analysis of under what circumstances a basically intensional predicate could be extensionalized. That this is an issue in itself casts doubt on their use of the extensionalizing meaning postulate, since meaning postulates are supposed to apply to lexical items without regard to the context of particular sentences. In contrast, reference to context is expected if what is at issue is, as I argue, the existence of pragmatic presuppositions. I see no way that G&S's analysis can accommodate the range of facts I have discussed without referring to context, but if that is so, then the introduction of a separate lexical distinction, intensionality *vs.* extensionality, beyond the factivity distinction, which is presupposition-based, hence susceptible to contextual influences, seems at best otiose. (Moreover, since intensional predicates are basic for G&S, *i.e.* the meaning postulate takes intensional predicates and extensionalizes them, we would appear to have the unappealing (though certainly not unprecedented) situation of a meaning postulate having to apply to most members of the lexical class it is meant to constrain, since the majority of *wh*-clause-embedding predicates seems able to have a factive reading (subject to context).)

5.3.2 Boër: Factivity Nullification

In contrast to G&S's analysis, Boër's (1978) approach is to treat *wh*-clauses as in effect denoting true propositions, like Karttunen does (*cf.* chapter II, note 8). In other words, the relation between the matrix predicate and the embedded *wh*-clause is taken to be basically factive.

The challenge for Boër, then, is to deal with cases where this assumed basic factivity is nullified, *i.e.* where the complement is not presupposed. We saw in chapter II that he appeals to lexical decomposition to handle *wonder* (*cf.* (19)). But his more general strategy is to develop a mechanism of factivity nullification, which is essentially the converse of G&S's extensionalizing meaning postulate, that is, it in effect intensionalizes the embedded clause. Boër in fact suggests that there is a lexical reflection of this operation in prepositions such as *about, at, as to, concerning*. He detects evidence for this in the following pair of sentences (1978(32-3)):

(73) a. John told me who had the winning number.
      b. John told me about who had the winning number.

He says that (73.a) entails that John told the truth, but (73.b) does not. I happen not to share his intuition here; for me, truth is entailed in both cases, though there is a difference, in that the first sentence entails that John in some way identified the winner, while in the second he need only have said something about the winner, without actually directly identifying him. Be that as it may, there are other cases where the addition of a preposition clearly does not nullify factivity, such as *know about, find out about, learn about*. Also, the verbs of surprise and (dis)pleasure (63.u,v) all can (and some must) take a preposition, but that does not nullify the factivity. There are, however, cases where I agree with Boër: *guess at* can I think only be understood nonfactively; on the other hand, I have argued that *guess* can be understood in both ways, even though there is no preposition. At the other end, both *speculate* and *speculate about* seem to me to have only a nonfactive use; Boër notes the same for *agree, debate*, and *decide* (though I disagree with him on the latter, cf. my discussion of (62.b)) and thus suggests that *about* can be abstractly present when it is not overt (I personally do not accept *decide about*, though *make a decision as to* is fine). Finally, the verbs *wonder* and *ask*, which only have a nonfactive understanding with an embedded *wh*-clause, seem to be able to get a factive reading precisely when combined with *about* (at least with an adjunct *if*-clause; *cf.* (70.a,b)). It seems, in short, that there is no empirically well-supported correlation between the presence *vs.* absence of certain prepositions with the matrix predicate and the interpretation of the *wh*-clause as presupposed or not.

Still, the idea of factivity nullification does not in and of itself depend on there being such a lexically marked indicator and the apparent predominance of a (possibly contextually conditioned) factive reading among *wh*-clause-embedding predicates makes such nullification prima facie more plausible than "factivity effectuation" as on G&S's account. Nevertheless, the same question of when to apply the operation is raised for Boër and for G&S, and again, my suspicion is that the role of context, concomitant with an appeal to pragmatic presupposition, renders strictly semantic operations superfluous.

5.4 Interrogative Structures

There is, however, a kind of construction that might indeed be regarded as a lexical manifestation of factivity-nullification; namely, what Baker (1968) called interrogative structures. These are sentences in which a basically factive predicate is embedded under another predicate, with the result that the complement of the factive predicate is now not presupposed. As evidence for this, Baker observed that if the complement of the embedded factive is a *that*-clause, which should otherwise be presupposed, the sentence is odd, whereas if the complement is a *wh*-clause, the sentence is unobjectionable:

(74) a. !John wanted to know that Bill cheated on the exam.
     b. John wanted to know who cheated on the exam.
(75) a. !Mary tried to discover that Bill ate the last cupcake.
     b. Mary tried to discover who ate the last cupcake.
(76) a. !Jane persuaded George to find out that Sue was at the party.
     b. Jane persuaded George to find out who was at the party.

If such interrogative structures are indeed a locus of factivity-nullification, we should expect the *wh*-clause not to be able to restrict an adverb of quantification; and this appears to be the case:

(77) a. The principal mostly wanted to find out which students cheated on the final exam.
     b. The principal mostly tried to find out which students cheated on the final exam.

    c.   The principal mostly persuaded Bill to find out which students cheated on the final exam.

None of these seems to me to be understandable as saying: "For most students who cheated on the final exam...." Rather, as in (the nonpresuppositional reading of) the sentences in (42), the *wh*-clause is just presenting the possibilities. It seems, then, that these interrogative structures are indeed an instance of lexically conditioned factivity-nullification. There still remains the question of just what constitutes an interrogative structure, but I will not undertake to answer that question here.

5.5 *A Loose End:* Tell

    Finally, I wish to return to the predicate we started this section off with, *tell*. This verb (and some, but not all, related verbs of communication), seems to have a number of odd properties that do not fall out straightforwardly from an appeal to pragmatic presupposition or any simple account based on factivity nullification (at least for my intuitions about sentences such as those in (73)). For one thing, although typically nonfactive when embedding a *that*-clause (but not if it's negated, *cf.* (64)), *tell* is apparently only factive when embedding a *wh*-clause; at least, I have been able to come up with no examples where I do not understand the *wh*-complement as presupposed (Grewendorf (1983) claims to get such a reading, but I do not share his intuition, which would actually accord better with my analysis than my own judgment). The only other predicates that behave similarly are those taken to be basically factive, such as *know* and *find out*. What about *tell* as part of an interrogative structure? Consider the following sentences:

(78) a.   John wanted to tell the principal who cheated on the final exam.
       b.   Mary tried to tell Sue who ate the last cupcake.
       c.   Jane persuaded George to tell Bill who was at the party.

In each of these sentences it seems to me that the *wh*-clause is presupposed, at least assuming that John knows who cheated on the final exam, Mary knows who ate the last cupcake, and George knows who was at the party, which seems natural. If, however, the object of telling is made the matrix subject, it does seems that the *wh*-clause is now not presupposed (although of the resulting sentences only (79.a) is perfectly fine, while (79.c) is virtually ungrammatical):

(79) a. The principal wanted to be told who cheated on the final exam.
   b. ?Sue tried to be told who ate the last cupcake.
   c. ?*Bill was persuaded to be told who was at the party.

This is presumably the case because all certainty of knowledge has been removed, which is not the case in (78), and (presumed) knowledge is the prerequisite for pragmatic presupposition. Aside from these cases, however, it does appear that the *wh*-complement of *tell* is always presupposed, which seems to conflict with the otherwise indifferent status of *tell* with respect to factivity. As a final, rather peculiar, example, which might contradict this conclusion, consider the contrast between the following two sentences:

(80) a. John told us which students the principal found out cheated on the final exam.
   b. The principal found out which students John told us cheated on the final exam.

Both compound clauses headed by the *wh*-phrase are presupposed here, but notice that the complement of *tell* in (80.b) is not in fact presupposed (that of *find out* in (80.a) is, but *find out* is basically factive). The point here is that the *wh*-phrase is associated with the subject gap in the deepest clause, *i.e.* this clause could be regarded as a *wh*-clause in the underlying syntactic representation. This would then be a case where the *wh*-complement of *tell* is not presupposed (aside from the passivized interrogative structures)—but only when the *wh*-phrase has been extracted out of the clause. I have no account of this state of affairs, if it is indeed the way it seems to be. (Incidentally, if the complement of *tell* in (80.b) is considered a *wh*-clause, that would be another problem for Boër's analysis, since there is apparently nothing to trigger factivity nullification here.)

5.6 Summary

We have seen that, in many cases, the quantifiability of embedded *wh*-phrases is pragmatically determined in that it is correlated with the (largely pragmatic) variability of many predicates with respect whether they presuppose their complement, *i.e.*, whether they have a factive interpretation. If they do (or can), then, in the logical representation, the complement is accommodated into the restrictive term, thus sanctioning quantification. The crucial role of context raises problems for more strictly semantic accounts such as Groenendijk and Stokhof's, according to which it is inherent properties of the matrix predicate that makes the difference, or Boër's, according to which *wh*-clauses are inherently factive. Nevertheless, while I think Boër's general approach is wrong, his strategy of factivity nullification does, in a number of cases, have some plausibility, as in Baker's interrogative structures.

6   Recapitulation

In this chapter I have given a nonquantificational logicosemantic analysis of *wh*-phrases. That is, *wh*-phrases are not inherently associated with a quantificational force, but are treated logically as open sentences, expressions containing an essential free variable. The primary empirical motivation for this is that they display quantificational variability under adverbs of quantification. This variability is neatly accounted for within the LHK theory of quantification, if the *wh*-clause itself is part of the restrictive term of the quantifier. I showed that there is considerable independent evidence for this semantic function of *wh*-clauses. I also proposed a general derivation of the the restrictive term by presupposition accommodation from the nuclear scope (essentially adopting ideas from Heim (1983b)), and showed how this accounts for a quantificational asymmetry among *wh*-clause-embedding predicates. Finally, I showed that many predicates display pragmatic variability regarding whether or not they presuppose their complement, and hence, whether or not embedded *wh*-clauses display quantificational variability; and I argued that an account along these lines is preferrable to one that bases the distinction on purely semantic properties, either of the embedding predicates or of the *wh*-clauses.

In chapter V I will pursue my analysis of the *wh*-clauses, concentrating on asymmetries between indefinites and *wh*-phrases, in particular syntactic environments where the latter fail to display quantificational variability: under nonpresupposing verbs, and as matrix clauses (direct questions). But before that, it is appropriate to evaluate my analysis against claims that the interpretation of *wh*-clauses involves exhausting the domain of discourse with respect to which it is evaluated; this is the subject of the next chapter.

Notes

1. The claim that *wh*-phrases and indefinites are logicosemantically similar is of course not new. Within generative grammar, *wh*-phrases were treated by Katz and Postal (1964) as consisting underlyingly of an indefinite NP plus a question morpheme; and Karttunen (1977) translates them as existentially quantified phrases, just like the classical analysis of indefinites. Moreover, the empirical justification for a parallel treatment of the two phrase types is supported by the fact that in many languages the same word (*e.g.* in Korean) or at least the same root (*e.g.* in Japanese) can serve both functions (*cf. e.g.* Kim (1989)); and in other languages, a *wh*-word may (or must) be used instead of an indefinite in certain syntactic environments, as in the following German and Latin examples (taken from von Stechow (1989, 24):

(i)   Da hat wer/jemand angerufen.
       There has who/someone called
(ii)   Si quis habet asinum, pulsat eum.
       If who has (a) donkey, (he) beats it

By drawing attention to quantificational parallels between the two phrase types, I am adding to the stockpile. But more important are the theoretical consequences, and that is why I go to such lengths to show how *wh*-constructions can be incorporated into the LHK theory.

2. The claim that *wh*-phrases display variable quantificational force under adverbs of quantification was first made in print, to my knowledge, by Nishigauchi (1986), who acknowledges David Pesetsky for suggesting the possibility. The Japanese constructions Nishigauchi is chiefly concerned with are certain kinds of relative clauses, *e.g.* concessive and free relatives; he also briefly considers concessive clauses in English (on free relatives in English, *cf.* section 3.3 below). The observation of *wh*-phrase quantificational variability in complement clauses (*i.e.*, indirect questions) was made by Angelika Kratzer, in Spring 1988 lectures at the University of Massachusetts, Amherst. Comorovski (1989, 48-49) also gives some examples, in the context of a discussion of *wh*-phrases and donkey anaphora, referring to a 1987 talk by Tanya

Reinhart (though Reinhart's examples involve only universal quantificational force).

3. Some of these sentences have a reading in which the adverb appears to quantify over events, situations, or occasions; I will return to this in chapter IV, section 2. In addition, (25.c) has another reading, in which the indefinite has existential force; this is due to its remaining in the nuclear scope of the quantifier. I will discuss in chapter V, section 3.1, an account of the conditions under which one or the other or both readings are available.

4. There are actually several difficulties with this assumption. One is that the presumed parallel with indefinites is not really there. I pointed out in chapter I, section 2.1, that the "default" universal force of an indefinite in an *if*-clause has been attributed by Heim (1982) to the semantics of the sentence as a whole, involving conditonal necessity. Such an interpretation is hardly available for (25.e). Nor is there a generic interpretation in this case. A second, even more problematic, difficulty is that it is not always the case that embedded *wh*-phrases have universal force when there is no explicit matrix adverb: there are examples of the kind pointed out by Hintikka where the *wh*-phrase is ambiguous between universal and existential force, as in (17) from chapter II. I have no explanation for this sort of ambiguity, though I am inclined to believe it is connected with modality, which, if so, might enable reestablishing the parallel with indefinites. This is an issue that needs more work than I can give it in the present study. All the examples without an explicit adverb of quantification that I use either only have, or at least favor, the universal reading, and I will simply assume, for simplicity, that it arises via a default universal quantifier.

5. As noted in chapter I, note 2, I will generally ignore the singular/plural distinction. However, in appendix B, I will suggest an approach to it, but the additional complication I discuss there plays no central role in the main points of my analysis, so I relegate it to the appendix.

6. It will be noticed that I have used singular indefinites in place of the plural *wh*-phrases in (25). In many cases, a plural indefinite seems to favor an existential intepretation, though I think the quantificational interpretation is sometimes possible. I do not know why this tendency, if generally true, is so; perhaps it is connected with the overall genericity of these sentences, such that a singular indefinite, in a

sense picking out an arbitrary individual, is more easily understood as representing a generalization about that individual than is a plural indefinite, which picks out a group. But groups can be generalized about too, so the preference for singular may have nothing to do with this. The reason the *wh*-phrases there are plural has to do with presupposition; I return to this in appendix B.

7. In Berman (1990) I failed to properly distinguish between adjunct and complement *if*-clauses, and consequently made the false claim that the latter can serve as restrictive terms of a quantifier.

8. This means that the *if*-clauses themselves must be divided into "restrictive term" and "nuclear scope," although strictly speaking not quantified structures. See Kadmon (1987), Kratzer (1989), and Diesing (1990b) for discussion of and argumentation for this process.

9. The literature on free relatives is quite large; they were distinguished by Jespersen (1961[1928]), though the name is apparently due to Ross (1967, 38); see Baker (1968), Grimshaw (1977), Bresnan and Grimshaw (1978), Groos and van Riemsdijk (1979) for classical transformational treatments; Jacobson (1988) is a recent discussion.

10. This fact was observed by Kratzer (1988), as a problem for the analysis of Jacobson (1988), who argues for a universal of free relatives, à la Karttunen's analysis of *wh*-questions.

11. *Cf.* Lees (1960, 60), quoted by Baker (1968, 15): "A sentence like: I know what he knows. is ambiguous; the Question-Word Factive Nominal [indirect question] has a meaning like that of: If he knows X, then I know he knows X., while the elliptic Relative Clause [free relative] sentence of the same shape has a meaning like that of: If he knows X, then I know X." *Cf.* also Strawson (1974).

12. The notion of presupposition intended here seems to be what is usually called pragmatic presupposition, as distinct from logical, or semantic, presupposition (according to which the truth of a proposition p is necessary for the truth of falsity of an utterance of which p is the presupposition). At any rate, this is the notion I will use in my analysis. The basic idea of pragmatic presupposition is that

> presuppositions are requirements that sentences, or utterances of sentences, place of sets of common background assumptions built up among conversational participants. Typically, the requirement is that this set of assumptions contain a specific proposition, or some proposition from

> a limited range of alternatives. Presuppositions in this
> sense are essentially things taken for granted at a given
> point in the conversation. (Soames (1989, 556))

This conception derives largely from the work of Stalnaker (e.g. 1972, 1974). It is sometimes subdivided into notions of speaker presupposition and utterance presupposition (*cf.* Soames (1982)), but for our purposes this distinction can be ignored. An important point is that pragmatic presuppositions can include semantic presuppositions: "Presupposition is, first and foremost, a matter of what is assumed or taken for granted [by language users] ....[but this] does not rule semantic explanations of pragmatic facts." (Soames (1989, 570))

13. This idea is formally developed within the LHK theory in Heim (1983b), in terms of a context-change semantics. For my purposes it is not necessary to go into the formal machinery of this theory, it is sufficient simply to show the effect on the logical representation.

14. Hintikka (1976) called the existential closure of the open sentence that corresponds to what I am calling the restrictive term the presupposition of the question (he was speaking here particularly of his treatment of direct questions). I am dispensing with existential closure (which in any case in the LHK theory applies only to the nuclear scope) and taking the open sentence itself to be the presupposition— not, though, of the "question", or the *wh*-clause, but of the nuclear scope. The analogy with Hintikka's analysis should not be given too much weight; in particular, Hintikka makes no attempt to derive his translations from presuppositional properties of the nuclear scope in the way I am doing (except for his reference to success presuppositions, noted in chapter II).

15. Roger Higgins pointed out (p.c.) that there is a similarity between my use of presuppositions and what McCawley (1979) called telescoping. McCawley proposes that the following two sentences have the same logical representations:

(i)   McGovern criticized Nixon for what he said to the Knights of Columbus.

(ii)   McGovern criticized Nixon for saying to the Knights of Columbus what he said to them.

McCawley also noted that Elliott's (1971) analysis of exclamatives works along the same lines:

(iii)   It's amazing the books that John has read. (=...that John has
         read the books that he has read)

Although these aren't quantified sentences, notice that the matrix predicates are factive. (In fact, it seems clear that telescoping is really what Heim (1983b) calls global accommodation, while in the case of quantified sentences we have local accommodation; *cf.* note 17 below.)

    16. There is a presuppositional difference between (25.a) and (29.a), having to do with the *which*-phrase; I return to this in appendix B.

    17. In terms of the context-change theory of Heim (1983b), mentioned in note 13, this sort of accommodation is what she calls local accommodation (*Cf.* (1983b, 120)): "rather like adjusting the context only for the immediate purpose of evaluating the constituent sentence." There is also what Heim calls global accommodation, *i.e.* accommodation to the level of the conversational context, not just to that of the immediate constituent; the accommodation of the *that*-clause in (45.a) is an instance of this. I will make crucial use of global accommodation in appendix B to deal with the effect of definiteness.

    18. In conditional assertions (*cf.* Belnap (1970), referred to at the beginning of section 4.1) the *if*-clause has been treated in effect as a presupposition of the consequent, *i.e.* the nuclear scope in terms of the LHK theory. Thus, where (A/B) represents the translation of a conditional assertion, Belnap gives the following rough semantic rule: If A is true, then what (A/B) asserts is what B asserts; if A is false, then (A/B) is nonassertive. As Quine put is (cited by Belnap): "If, after we have made such an affirmation [of 'if A then B'], the antecedent turns out to be true, then we consider ourselves committed to the consequent... If on the other hand the antecedent turns out to have been false, our conditional affirmation is as if it had never been made." (The notion of presupposition implicit here is the logical, not pragmatic, one; however, the point being made is essentially the same.)

    19. The translation of the subject NP, *a cat*, must of course be part of the restrictive term to yield the correct interpretation. This does not happen here by presupposition accommodation, since indefinites are not presupposed (*cf.* Heim (1982)). However, as a rule the subject

NP is part of the restrictive term in the logical translation. In chapter V I will present a theory of the mapping from syntax to logical form that accounts for this observation. (Although I have not represented the translation of *a cat* in the nuclear scope as well as in the restrictive term in (49), there would be no harm in doing so; it is merely redundant.)

20. *Cf.* German *abwarten* (Hölker (1981)).

21. I myself tend to restrict *acknowledge* to a factive meaning, *i.e.* more like *admit* than *confess*.

22. The following quotation (from Penrose (1989, 387)) is a nice example of this ambiguity; it concerns a neurological patient, D.B., with a partially damaged visual cortex, who experienced blindsight, *i.e.* the ability to process visual information without being conscious of seeing: "However, when something was placed in this region [i.e. of the impaired visual field] and D.B. was asked to *guess* what that something was..., he found he could do so with near to 100 per cent accuracy!" The first occurrence of *guess* is clearly nonpresuppositional, the second (ellipted) one, clearly presuppositional (and, moreover, the ellipted *wh*-clause is quantified by the adverbial phrase *with near to 100 per cent accuracy*).

IV

Exhaustiveness

1 Introduction

Recall from chapter II that the analyses of Karttunen (1977) and Groenendijk and Stokhof (1982;1984;1989) in effect associate *wh*-phrases with universal force, by requiring that the *wh*-clause denote all true propositions formed by assigning a value to the *wh*-phrase (for G&S the restriction to true propositions holds only for extensional predicates). In contrast, the Åqvist/Hintikka analysis associates *wh*-phrases with existential as well as universal force. The analysis I have presented in chapter III takes this widening of the quantificational possibilities to its logical conclusion by allowing *wh*-phrases to be associated with the whole range of quantificational forces, in consequence of which *wh*-phrases are treated as inherently nonquantificational. The basic evidence for this approach is the interpretation of sentences such as those in (25) in chapter III, in which, as I argue, the *wh*-phrases are quantified by adverbs of quantification, just as are indefinites on the LHK theory.

In this chapter I want to examine how the evidence that motivates my analysis bears on the claims of universal force put forth by Karttunen and G&S. These claims have become known under the rubric of exhaustiveness, following the position originally enunciated by Baker (1968). Implicit in Baker's discussion, and made explicit by G&S (1982), are in fact two notions of exhaustiveness, that differ with regard to whether just the positive extension of the embedded predicate is taken to contribute to the interpretation of the *wh*-clause, or both the positive and negative extensions. Following Bäuerle and Zimmermann (1987, 28), I will refer to the former as weak and the latter as strong exhaustiveness.[1] According to the weaker notion, it suffices to consider values for the *wh*-phrase that satisfy the embedded clause in a sentence such as *John knows who left.*, while according to the stronger notion values must in addition be considered that satisfy the negation of that clause; in both cases exhaustiveness entails that all values must be satisfying. In section 2 of this chapter I will show that weak exhaustiveness is not an inherent property of *wh*-clauses, which is a direct consequence of the quantificational variability of *wh*-phrases, as amply illustrated in chapter III. In particular, I will try to refute arguments that the evidence from that chapter can be interpreted in a way that preserves exhaustiveness. In section 3 I will discuss strong exhaustiveness: first, I will show that, again because of quantificational variability, there is no inherent exhaustiveness; then I will argue at length that the notion of strength, which essentially has to do with the size domain of quantification relevant for interpretation, is in general at odds with the linguistic facts, and that reference to the positive extension of the embedded predicate is all that is generally required (section 3.1). Finally, I will discuss (section 3.2) a side-effect of my analysis, that it ignores false information, and suggest that unwanted consequences of this are avoided as a result of a kind of Gricean conversational implicature.

2   (Weak) Exhaustiveness

Baker viewed the question-answer relation similarly to Karttunen and G&S, that is, he took questions to have (no more than) one true complete (semantic) answer each. Thus the question-answer relation must be what he called exhaustive, in the following way (1968, 36):

> Let us use the term "partial answer" to refer to any true sentence satisfying the schema provided by the question, or any conjunction of such sentences. We then say that a partial answer to a question "satisfies the exhaustiveness condition" with respect to that question if it is possible to deduce from that partial answer any and all other partial answers, provided we are furnished with information about relations of synonymy existing between individual

words and about the reference intended by proper names
and descriptions.

Exhaustiveness in this sense entails, for example, that, at an index, a
wh-question is associated with all its true answers. Baker admitted that
the effect of the exhaustiveness condition "is not readily apparent" with
direct questions (p.34), but noted that with indirect questions exhaustiveness accounts for the perceived contradiction in a sentence such as the
following (p.35(3.14)):

(81)   John knows who is running, but he doesn't know that George is
       running.

The *that*-clause counts as a partial true answer (true because the matrix
verb is factive), so if the *wh*-clause denotes (the set of propositions
containing, or the single proposition consisting of the conjunction of)
all its true answers, then (81) entails that John both knows and does
not know the proposition denoted by the *that*-clause. Because of this
dependence of the interpretation of the *wh*-clause, I will say that it is
being understood exhaustively, or simply, that it is exhaustive.

Another way of illustrating the supposed exhaustiveness of
indirect *wh*-questions is given by G&S (1982), in the form an inference
schema, which recalls a syllogism; the following is an example:

(82)   John knows who is running.
       George is running.
       John knows that George is running.

From the truth of the two premises in (82) the truth of the conclusion
is to follow; weak exhaustiveness entails that all similar arguments, in
which the second premise is replaced by a true sentence of the same
form and the conclusion correspondingly changed, are valid. In other
words, weak exhaustiveness entails the validity of the following argument:

(83)   John knows who is running.
       Of every individual who is running, John knows that s/he is run-
       ning.

While I agree that the sentence in (81) seems contradictory and
the argument in (82) seems valid, consider the following:

(84)   John mostly knows who is running, but he doesn't know that
       George is running.
(85)   John mostly knows who is running.
       George is running.
       ―――――――――――――――――――――――
       John knows that George is running.

In contrast to (81) and (82), (84) does not seem contradictory to me and
I think the premises of the argument in (85) can be true without the
conclusion being true. I would like to conclude from this that exhaustiveness is not an inherent property of *wh*-clauses, despite the existence of
examples such as (81) and (82).

    It might be objected, however, that (84) and (85) are not really
of the same form as (81) and (82), respectively, so cannot be used to
argue against them. In particular, in each of the former examples the
adverb *mostly* occurs in the sentence embedding the *wh*-clause, but not
in the sentence embedding the *that*-clause, while there is no adverb in
either of the latter examples. Since *mostly* is a sentential operator, if
its occurrence is taken to refute exhaustiveness, for instance by invali-
dating the argument in (85), then so should that of the negation, also a
sentential operator, in the following argument (Angelika Kratzer, p.c.):

(86)   John doesn't know who is running.
       George is running.
       ―――――――――――――――――――――――
       John knows that George is running.

It seems clear, however, that the invalidity of (86) has no bearing on
the question of exhaustiveness.

    I think that this type of objection can be countered by taking
care to distinguish between intuitions about the meaning of sentences
and the logical analysis given to a sentence. The sentences and arguments in (81)-(85) are not logical translations but pieces of natural
language about which we have intuitions, which we would like a
logical analysis to accurately reflect. In terms of my analysis, as presented in chapter III, the argument in (85), for example, would take the
following form (assume, for convenience, that x is a variable over
people):

(87)   MOST [be-running'(x)] [know'(j,[be-running'(x)])]
       is-running'(g)
       know'(j,be-running'(g))

And the argument in (82) would translate to the following, assuming that the absence of an explicit quantifier in a sentence with an indirect question indicates the default implicit universal quantifier in the logical translation:

(88)   ALL [be-running'(x)] [know'(j,[be-running'(x)])]
       is-running'(g)
       know'(j,be-running'(g))

Now the argument in (88) is valid according to usual assumptions about logical inference: since the first premise is a universal proposition, we can consider any substitution value for x as an instance: in particular, g (*i.e.*, George). Then by a version of modus ponens, appropriately formulated for restricted quantification, the argument goes through. In (87), on the other hand, universal instantiation cannot apply, since the quantifier is not a universal, so the inference fails. In short, although (84) and (85) differ superficially from (81) and (82), respectively, they have (I claim) the same kind of logical form, so it is appropriate to consider them in evaluating the question of exhaustiveness. This is further supported by the following argument:

(89)   Without exception, John knows who is running.
       George is running.
       John knows that George is running.

This argument, in which the first premise has an explicit universal adverb of quantification, has the translation in (88) on my analysis, and it is just as valid as (82), which supports the use of the implicit universal quantifier in the translation of the latter.

While I thus maintain that examples such as (84) and (85) can be used to evaluate exhaustiveness, and then they argue against exhaustiveness, another interpretation of such examples might be suggested (as I was reminded in this connection by Roger Schwarzschild) that seems to allow upholding exhaustiveness. Consider the following example:

(90)   The principal usually finds out which students cheat on the final
       exam, but she didn't find out that Bill cheated on the final exam.

The first conjunct of (90), so runs this argument, does not have the
interpretation that my analysis assigns it, on which individuals are
quantified over, yielding a meaning paraphrased as: for most students
cheat on the final exam the principal finds out of them that they cheat
on the final exam. Instead, this sentence is argued to involve quantification over situations, specifically final-exam-situations. The interpretation of the *wh*-clause is further taken to be exhaustive, so that the
interpretation of the whole sentence is paraphrased as: in most final-
exam-situations *s*, for all students who cheat in *s*, the principal finds
out of them that they cheat in *s*. On this interpretation, the sentence in
(90) is not contradictory if the final exam that Bill cheated on is not
one of those of which the principal found out which students cheated
on it, since (90) would not be claiming that the principal found out
about student cheating on all the final exams but only most of them.
       What this argument shows, it seems to me, is not so much the
possibility of maintaining *wh*-clause exhaustiveness as the probable
necessity to consider situations as entities that adverbs of quantification
can quantify over. I do believe that some notion of situations is likely
to play a role in the correct analysis of certain properties of sentences
with adverbs of quantification—I have argued along these lines in
Berman (1987)—but even so, I think that the case for exhaustiveness is
not saved.[2] Consider the following situation: suppose that for every
final exam the principal finds out of at least 60% of the students who
cheat on it that they cheat on it, but that for no single final does she
find out of all the students who cheat on it that they cheat on it, and in
particular, she does not find out that Bill cheated on the one that he
took. Notice that I have built nonexhaustiveness into this situation;
yet I think that (90) is an accurate report of it. This seems to clearly
show that *wh*-clauses need not be exhaustive, even if situations are
quantified over. The point can also be made by an appropriately modi-
fied sentence on the pattern of (90):

(91)   For every final exam, the principal usually finds out which
       students cheat on it, but for no final exam does she find out
       without exception which students cheat on it.

Intuitively, there is no contradiction here; nor is there on my analysis, as is seen in the following translation (without a situation variable), the nuclear scopes of whose two major conjuncts are clearly compatible:[3]

(92) ALL [final-exam'(x)] [MOST [student'(y) & cheat-on'(y,x)]]
      [find-out'(tp,[student'(y) & cheat-on'(y,x)])]] &
      ALL [final-exam'(x)] [NOT [ALL [student'(y) & cheat-on'(y,x)]
      [find-out'(tp,[student'(y) & cheat-on'(y,x)])]]]]

Aside from the fact, just demonstrated, that *wh*-clause exhaustiveness may fail to obtain even when a reasonable case may be made for quantifying over situations, there are examples where the appeal to situations seems less plausible, and where there can be no question of exhaustiveness. The sentences in (84) and (85) are cases in point: they are perfectly compatible with being uttered in a situation where there is just one election, and John is being reported to know most of the candidates, but he is not being reported to know all of them. (If it is suggested that the appropriate situation is not an election, but the running of candidates for office, then the most likely scenario is where each running-situation contains one candidate, which is the same thing as quantifying over the individual candidates, as on my analysis.) The sentences in (25.b,e) of chapter III are even less plausible candidate for quantifying over situations, since the simple past with achievement and accomplishment predicates generally makes the sentence aspect episodic, *i.e.* about a single episode or situation; this can be effectively forced by adding a limiting temporal modifier:

(93) a. Sue mostly remembers which of her birthday presents last
          year arrived special delivery.
      b. John discovered which books were stolen from the library
          yesterday.

In sum, I have argued that *wh*-clauses are not inherently exhaustive, in the sense that they are supposed to denote the set (or conjunction) of all propositions that result from substitution of the free variable in the translation of the *wh*-phrase. The evidence for my argument is the quantificational variability seen in sentences such as those in (25) from chapter III, which I take to show that *wh*-phrases are not associated with an inherent quantificational force. The arguments of Baker, Karttunen, and G&S in favor of exhaustiveness, which have some intuitive force, were shown to be amenable to a logical treatment in terms of my analysis, according to which they point to no more than the presence of an implicit universal quantifier; whereas, if similar arguments, but with a less than universal quantifier, are made, then intuitively (and on my analysis) there is no appearance of exhaustiveness. The possibility of retaining exhaustiveness through quantifying over situations was shown not to work in general, either because it is possible to construct nonexhaustive situations in which the sentences in question are still intuitively true, or because there are cases where the only plausible situation-variable has just one instantiation, which is incompatible with quantifiers that require multiple instantiations for truth: in such cases, the simplest alternative that yields the correct truth conditions is simply to quantify over the variable of the *wh*-phrase, but then the *wh*-clause itself cannot in general be exhaustive, in the weak sense. As for the strong sense, this is what I examine next.

3 The Domain of Quantification

As I said in section 1, strong exhaustiveness is an extension of weak exhaustiveness into the negative extension of the predicate of *wh*-clause; that is, weak exhaustiveness as it obtains with the negation of this predicate. Thus, strong exhaustiveness entails the validity of both the following argument and its inverse:

(94)   John knows who ran.
        John knows who did not run.

Another way of putting this is that, whereas analysing *wh*-clauses as weakly exhaustive is equivalent to identifying their logical translations with universal conjunctions of *that*-clauses, strong exhaustiveness is equivalent to identifying them with universal conjunctions of *whether*-clauses. This would account for the anomaly Baker perceives in the following sentence (1968, 50(4.19))), as he pointed out:

(95)   The senator knows who voted for the bill, but he doesn't know whether or not Peebles voted for the bill.

If the *wh*-clause is strongly exhaustive then this sentence is contradictory, since the first conjunct would entail that the senator knows of everyone whether or not he voted for the bill, thus in particular that he knows whether or not Peebles voted for the bill. (Contrast this with (81) above, whose contradictoriness is already accounted for by weak exhaustiveness.)

In this section I want to concentrate on the notion of strength involved in strong exhaustiveness, that is, on the claim that both the positive and the negative extension of the embedded predicate must be taken into account in evaluating sentences with an embedded *wh*-clause. As for the claim of exhaustiveness, this is no different than the case for weak exhaustiveness, and readily dispatched once the quantificational variability of *wh*-phrases is taken into account. Thus, for example, there is no sense of contradiction in the following sentence, whatever may be the case with (95) (I will argue below that the latter too has a noncontradictory reading, but this concerns the issue of strength, not exhaustiveness):

(96)   The senator mostly knows who voted for the bill, but he doesn't know whether or not Peebles voted for the bill.

The quantificational force of the first conjunct is less than universal, so it is compatible with the senator's not knowing whether Peebles voted or not. Thus, there is nothing new regarding the claim of exhaustiveness. The claim of strength, however, is qualitatively different from the weak claim (where only the positive domain of the embedded predicate is considered), and it is this that I wish to examine in detail. In order to emphasize the independence of the claim of strength from the claim of exhaustiveness, I will refer to the former as the strong domain hypothesis.

3.1 How Much is Enough?

We can see that the strong domain hypothesis is in principal independent of exhaustiveness by generalizing the inference pattern in (94) in the following way. Let us assume that the two sentences in this example are instances of implicit universal quantification. (Although this is not how G&S analyse it, this assumption does preserve the validity of the argument, which they cite as evidence of strong exhaustive-ness, so is innocuous, it seems to me; moreover, it is useful for the point in question.) Given this, (94) is quantificationally equivalent to the following argument:

(97)   John knows, without exception, who ran.
       John knows, without exception, who did not run.

If the same kind of strength-claim holds for less-than-universal quantifica-tional force, then the following argument is likewise predicted to be valid:

(98)   John mostly knows who ran.
       John mostly knows who did not run.

I think that this prediction is not borne out, but before elaborating on this I want to draw attention to a crucial assumption, necessary for the strong domain hypothesis to have the effect its proponents desire.

The validity of (94) and (97) (as well as the contradictoriness of (95)) only follows on the assumption that the individual denoted by the subject NP is completely aware of what makes up the domain of dis-course relevant for the embedded clause. If, for example, the domain relevant for (94)/(97) consists of Mary, George, Sue, and Bill, and only Mary and George ran, and John knows that they ran, and he knows that Sue did not run, but he doesn't even know that Bill is in the domain, then although the premise of (94)/(97) is true in this situation, the conclusion isn't. Let us call this assumption the complete awareness hypothesis. To reiterate, the strong domain hypothesis must be supple-mented with the complete awareness hypothesis in order for arguments such as (94)/(97) to be valid.[4,5]

G&S (1982) choose to exclude from their formal analysis "the type of situation in which the subject of the propositional attitude is not fully informed as to which set of individuals constitutes the domain of discourse" (cited from (1984, 87)). They note they could dispense with the complete awareness hypothesis, "for example by allowing the domain of discourse to vary with possible worlds" (*ibid.*, p.88); how-ever, they choose not to do this, because it raises "a number of well-known problems" which they regard as general to the possible-worlds framework, thus transcending the analysis of *wh*-clauses. These problems have to do with (among others) modelling situations that intuitively make no ascription of logical omniscience. (G&S discuss this issue further in their dissertation (1984, pp. 283, 405(n.33), 483, and 487-8).) But such situations are, I argue, the general case with respect to the interpretation of embedded *wh*-clauses, and therefore a formal analysis that a priori excludes this possibility (allowing it in only through changes in the structure of the model) should be viewed with skepticism. On my analysis, the complete awareness hypothesis is irrelevant, amounting to extra formal baggage; it could be added, say by meaning postulate under particular circumstances, but it is not an essential ingrediant of the general analysis. Moreover, as I will show directly, in many cases it (together with the strong domain hypothesis) leads to wrong predications. My evidence against it comes from sentences with less-than-universal force, and those whose matrix predicates are not of the *know*-type.[6]

Let us, thus, return to the argument in (98), and consider the following situation. Suppose the domain consists of ten individuals, seven of whom ran. We assume, for the sake of argument, the complete awareness hypothesis, *i.e.*, John knows of the existence of all ten people. Suppose that John knows of six of the seven who ran that they ran, while of the three who didn't run, he knows of only one that s/he didn't run; of the remaining three people, John doesn't know whether they ran or not. It seems to me that this situation is perfectly compatible with the sentence *John mostly knows who ran.*, but it is not compatible with *John mostly knows who didn't run*. But this means that (98) is an invalid argument. In other words, even granting the complete awareness hypothesis, the strong domain hypothesis makes intuitively incorrect predictions when applied to cases of less-than-universal quantificational force.

This conclusion can also be maintained in a great many cases where the quantificational force is universal. Consider arguments of the form in (94) (*i.e.* with implicit universal quantification) with a variety of matrix predicates other than *know*:

(99) a. John told Sue who ran.
          John told Sue who didn't run.
      b. Mary guessed who ran.
          Mary guessed who didn't run.

   c.   <u>Bill contemplated who ran.</u>
        Bill contemplated who didn't run.
   d.   <u>John wasn't surprised by who ran.</u>
        John was surprised by who didn't run.
   e.   <u>Sue was disappointed by who ran.</u>
        Sue was disappointed by who didn't run.
   f.   <u>Mary explained to us who ran.</u>
        Mary explained to us who didn't run.
   g.   <u>Bill confirmed who ran.</u>
        Bill confirmed who didn't run.

We may again freely assume the complete awareness hypothesis; nevertheless, it seems clear that these arguments are invalid. In each case, the subject's awareness of the domain is independent of her/his holding the attitude expressed by the matrix predicate. For example, even if John knows who constitutes those who ran as well as those who didn't run, it doesn't follow that his telling Sue who ran entails his telling Sue who didn't run; his act of telling is simply a positive act, *i.e.* made with respect to the positive extension of the embedded predicate. (If Sue is to infer who didn't run from his telling her who ran, then Sue must herself be aware of the negative extension, regardless of what John's awareness is.) The same reasoning obtains with the other examples in (99).

     Note that the matrix predicates in (99.a-c) are among the verbs usually classified as nonfactive but which, as I discussed in chapter III, section 5.2, can be understood factively. It is the factive reading that is at stake here, since, as shown in section 4.2 of chapter III, it is only on this interpretation that the *wh*-clause gets accommodated into the restrictive term, thus helping to determine the domain of quantification. (Karttunen (1977, 22) argues against the semantic equivalence resulting from strong exhaustiveness by pointing out the intuitive nonsynonymy of *Bill wonders who dates Mary.* and *Bill wonders who doesn't date Mary*; however, since *wonder* is a purely nonfactive verb, the example is not apposite.[7])

     In sum, I have shown that assuming the complete awareness hypothesis does not ensure the validity in general of arguments of the form in (94). There are two classes of counterexamples: cases in which the matrix predicate is not of the *know*-type, as in the examples in (99), and cases in which the quantificational force of the premise and conclusion are less than universal, as in (98). And, since, as G&S admit, the strong domain hypothesis in the absence of the complete awareness hypothesis is insufficient to ensure the validity of arguments for the claim of strength even in the universal case, I conclude that the claim of strength, *i.e.* the claim that the negative extension of the embedded predicate should be taken into consideration, does not generally hold. In other words, in interpreting sentences with an embedded *wh*-clause, all we need generally consider is the positive extension of the embedded predicate.[8]

3.2 How Much is Too Much?

If the preceding conclusion is correct, then it supports my analysis: since the restrictive term, which determines the domain of quantification, contains the translation of the *wh*-clause (as a result of presupposition accommodation) but not of its negation, only the positive extension of this clause contributes to the domain. But is this really enough? Consider the following situation, which appears to pose a problem for my analysis.[9] Suppose that exactly Sue, Bill, Dave, and Mary ran, but that John believes that Sue, Bill, Dave, Mary, and Jane ran. Is the sentence *John knows who ran.* true in this situation? According to my analysis it is, because for all people (again assuming implicit default universal quantification) who in fact ran, it is true that John knows of them that they ran, that is, both the restrictive term and the nuclear scope of the quantifier are evaluated as true. The case where John "knows"—*i.e.* believes—someone else ran, who in fact did not run, does not play a role in my analysis, because here the restrictive term is not satisfied, so the evaluation does not get off the ground.

I want to maintain the position that, as far as truthconditional semantics is concerned, my analysis is right—John does indeed know who ran in the above situation. This claim goes against what G&S (1982) call the intermediate exhaustiveness of *wh*-clauses, according to which the following inference pattern is valid:

(100) John believes that Bill and Mary ran.
       <u>Only Bill ran.</u>
       John does not know who ran.

Yet it seems to me that, in an objective sense, John does have the knowledge of who ran; he happens, in addition, to have a false belief about who ran. Thus, I think a different conclusion can be drawn from the first two premises in (100), namely, that John knows who ran but he does not know that he knows who ran.

This issue is a controversial one in epistemological theory, and I do not propose to enter into it at any length, but will confine myself, as in the previous subsection, to a consideration of linguistic intuitions with a variety of predicates. I should note, though, my conclusion is at odds with Hintikka (1962), who claimed to prove that, at least within his epistemic logic, knowing does entail knowing that one knows. However, Chisolm (1970[1963], 208) argues that all Hintikka really shows is "that if a man does not know that he knows that *p* (or perhaps does not *think* that he knows that *p*), then he should not say that he knows that *p*." Moreover, Radford (1970 [1966]) accepts that one can know without knowing that he knows, and uses this to argue that neither believing that *p*, being sure that *p*, nor being justified in being sure that *p*, are necessary conditions for knowing that *p* (thus, he professes to show the other direction to Gettier's famous argument (1963) that justified true belief is not sufficient grounds for knowledge).

With verbs of the *know*-type, it is always a question of whether the subject's beliefs are true or false; if enough of them are true then, even if some are false, I am arguing that this is sufficient to attribute knowledge (*e.g.*) of the complement to the subject, though not to attribute to her/him the knowledge that s/he knows this.[10] With many other verbs, however, the subject's beliefs do not necessarily play a role. Suppose that just Mary, Bill, and George ran, and that John knows this (thus also believes it). Yet John wanted to deceive Sue, but not by withholding facts from her, so he told her that Mary, Bill, George, and Sally ran. Still, in the objective sense referred to above, we can say that John told Sue who ran (contrast this with the situation where John told Sue that Sally, Dave, and Jane ran—then he certainly did not tell Sue who ran). Moreover, John knows that he told Sue who ran, although he also added false information (therefore, if John is Sue's only source as to who ran, although she would know who ran, she would not know that she knows this, exactly as in the preceding discussion of *know*). It might, instead, be the case that John does falsely believe that Sally ran, in addition to correctly believing that

Mary, Bill, and George ran, and on this basis tells Sue that Mary, Bill, George, and Sally ran. Again, he told Sue who ran, but this time, he doesn't know that he told her. Verbs of communication seem readily able to function in this way; each of the following examples can be (objectively) true, even if John (deceptively or mistakenly) adds false information:[11]

(101) a. John wrote down in his diary who ran.
     b. John discussed with us who ran.
     c. The gossip column published who ran.
     d. The manual lists where to send the appliance for repairs.

Other types of verbs can, I think, also participate in this paradigm, as in the following examples:

(102) a. John guessed who ran.
     b. John imagined who ran.
     c. John contemplated who ran.
     d. John anticipated who ran.

As long as what John guessed, imagined, contemplated, or anticipated includes the truth, these sentences are true.

    All of the examples in the preceding paragraph involve the same kind of matrix verbs as employed in the previous section, *i.e.* ones that are usually classified as nonfactive but can have factive interpretations. It is, of course, the factive interpretation that makes these examples true, but, perhaps, because a nonfactive interpretation is also possible, false information is not excluded, though it plays no role in the objective evaluation of these sentences. With the purely factive verbs, false information is also not excluded: as we have seen, the possibility of false information here is tied to the beliefs of the subject—and belief is prototypically nonfactive—and the concomitant possibility of not knowing that one knows.

    In short, again, I argue that all it takes for a sentence containing a *wh*-clause to be true is for the appropriate number of values (as determined by the quantification) for the *wh*-phrase(s) to be satisfied—false (*i.e.* nonsatisfying) values do not play a role, thus are not excluded. This leads to the possibility of someone knowing (*e.g.*) something without knowing that s/he knows it. In other words, I am holding that the objective facts of the situation are enough to evaluate the truth of these sentences.

Nevertheless, I acknowledge that there is a tendency to understand these sentences, especially if uttered out of the blue, as excluding false information. I would like to suggest that this understanding is a kind of Gricean conversational implicature. Here is Grice's (1975) characterization of this notion:

> A man who, by (in, when) saying (or making as if to say) that p has implicated that q, may be said to have conversationally implicated that q, provided that (1) he is to be presumed to be observing the conversational maxims, or at least the Cooperative Principle; (2) the supposition that he is aware that, or thinks that, q is required in order to make his saying or making as if to say p (or doing so in those terms) consistent with this presumption; and (3) the speaker thinks (and would expect the hearer to think that the speaker thinks) that it is within the competence of the hearer to work out, or grasp intuitively, that the supposition mentioned in (2) is required.

Let us see how this might work by applying it to the following sentence:

(103) John told us who ran.

I am proposing that someone who utters this sentence normally implicates that, for any individual in the domain who did not run, John did not tell us that that s/he ran. We may assume that Grice's conditions (1) and (3) are satisfied (*i.e.* that this is not a deviant conversation); the key to the implicature, then, is the satisfaction of condition (2). This follows, I think, from an interaction of parts of the four conversational maxims with the semantics of embedded *wh*-clauses. According to the latter, as shown in the previous subsection, false information (*i.e.*, values from the negative extension of the the embedded predicate) is irrelevant to the evaluation of a quantified sentence containing a *wh*-clause—this is the effect of rejecting the strong domain hypothesis. Now, speakers may be expected to make their utterances conform to the basic semantic rules of the language (this can be regarded as following from the Cooperative Principle). Thus, given the semantics, an utterance of (103) that was predicated on false information would constitute a violation of both the maxim of Relation (be relevant) and the first maxim of Quality (do not say what you believe to be false); hence the implicature that, ceteris paribus, what John told us contains no falsehoods.[12] Note that it is possible to explicitly exclude false information, for instance by saying "John told us who ran and didn't say that anyone ran who in fact did not run," but since this is already implicated by (103), such a circumlocution would have violated both the third maxim of Manner (be brief) and the second Quantity maxim (do not make your contribution more informative than is required).

Now one thing that can happen to implicatures is that they can be defeated, for instance if the context of utterance is incompatible with the implicature, but also by an explicit utterance that contradicts what is implicated. However, this explicit utterance should not contradict the utterance that carries the implicature itself: if it did, that would be evidence that it was not a conversational implicature, but an integral part of the truthconditional meaning. Now it seems to me that the following sentences are not contradictory, though they explicitly deny the kind of implicature derived in the previous paragraph:

(104) a. John knows who ran, though there are also some people he believes ran who did not in fact run.

b. John told us who ran, though there were also some people he mentioned who did not in fact run.

c. John wrote down in his diary who ran, though there were also some people he listed who did not in fact run.

d. John discussed with us who ran, though there were also some people he mentioned who did not in fact run.

e. The gossip column published who ran, though there were also some people it listed who did not in fact run.

f. John (correctly) guessed who ran, though there were also some people he guessed who did not in fact run.

g. John contemplated who ran, though there were also some people he thought about who did not in fact run.

h. John (correctly) anticipated who ran, though there were also some people he expected would run who in fact did not.

4 Summary

I have argued, first, that the evidence of *wh*-phrase quantificational variability is as it appears to be, and that *wh*-clauses not exhaustive. Even if situations can be quantified over, there are scenarios that exclude the exhaustive interpretation. Secondly, I have argued that only the positive extension of the embedded predicate need generally be taken into account in determining the truth of the quantification. This is supported by sentences involving less-than-universal quantificational force, as well as sentences that do not depend for their interpretation on the awareness of the matrix subject. Finally, I have argued that false information does not play a role in interpreting these sentences, but that there is, nevertheless, typically a conversational implicature to that effect, which can, however, be defeated.

Having refuted the arguments for an exhaustive interpretation of *wh*-clauses, and in so doing defended my nonquantificational analysis of *wh*-phrases, which is based on quantificational parallels between them and indefinites, I now turn, in the final chapter, to quantificational asymmetries between these two phrase types.

Notes

1. G&S (1982) also distinguish an intermediate degree of exhaustiveness; I return to this in section 3.2.

2. The issue alluded to here is the proportion problem, referred to in chapter 1, note 8. Again, I am ignoring that issue in this dissertation, since I believe that my main points are independent of it and that whatever turns out to be the best approach to this "problem" (more likely set of problems) can be added onto my basic analysis, as I think is the case with any kind of LHK analysis.

3. I have exported the negation in the second conjunct to its nuclear scope, so as to bring out the compatibility between MOST and NOT-ALL; the translation in (92) is logically equivalent to the following:

(i)   NOT [SOME [final-exam'(x)]
       [ALL [student'(y) & cheat-on'(y,x)]
       [find-out'(tp,[student'(y) & cheat-on'(y,x)])]]]]

This translation more naturally reflects the syntax of the English sentence.

4. A potential interpretation of (94) under which it would be valid without appeal to the complete awareness hypothesis is the following. If John knows that Mary and George are the only people who ran, then we may safely assume that he knows that everyone other than these two did not run, though he may not be able to identify these other people in any other way. If the conclusion in (94) can be understood in this way then the argument is valid. This is not, however, the usual assumption, and I will not be making it in my discussion. Note in particular that on this interpretation the inverse of (94) would not be valid, contrary to intended consequences of strong exhaustiveness.

5. The discussion and examples in G&S (1982) concerning strong exhaustiveness are in the context of an analysis of indirect questions. However, in later work (1984, ch.IV-VI) G&S analyse direct questions as also involving a claim of strength, so that, *e.g.*, *Who ran?* and *Who didn't run?* are semantically equivalent. The complete awareness hypothesis is, of course, not applicable to direct questions.

However, there seems to me little intuitive appeal to the strong domain hypothesis in the analysis of direct questions—certainly not as interrogatives utterances. In other words, I see no plausible linguistic reason for building strong exhaustiveness into the analysis of direct questions; it is, however, a formal consequence of G&S's treatment of questions as denoting partitions of the set of indices (*cf.* chapter II, section 4.2). (I return to direct *wh*-questions in chapter V.)

6. The conjunction of the strong domain and complete awareness hypotheses does not always make arguments of the form in (94) valid on G&S's analysis; in particular, not if the *wh*-phrases are *which*-phrases. These are treated in what G&S call a de dicto fashion, the effect of which is that the denotation of the *which*-phrase depends on the index of evaluation. Consequently, as long as the denotation of the noun of the *which*-phrase is contingent, the entire *wh*-clause will not be semantically equivalent to its negation. However, for *wh*-clauses containing *who*-phrases rather than *which*-phrases, this equivalence does obtain on their analysis. In my examples I have therefore used *who*-phrases to emphasize that, nevertheless, the strong domain and complete awareness hypotheses do not in general produce intuitively correct results.

7. G&S treat *wonder* as an intensional predicate (*cf.* chapter II, section 4.2), so it does not induce weak exhaustiveness on their account. It appears, however, that in terms of G&S's formal analysis, if I understand it, *wh*-clauses are nevertheless strongly exhaustive under an intensional predicate. The reason is basically same as with extensional predicates on their analysis. The sense or propositional concept denoted by, *e.g.*, *who didn't run* is a function that for each index k yields the set of indices i such that the individuals who didn't run at k are the same as those who didn't run at i; for each k this function picks out the same set of indices as picked out by the sense of *who ran*, because at any index, the set of runners and the set of nonrunners together exhaust the domain of individuals (*cf.* chapter II, note 18). In other words, in each case the subject stands in the wonder-relation to the same propositional concept. This indicates that strong exhaustiveness is not simply a strengthening of weak exhaustiveness on G&S's account.

8. For verbs of the *know*-type, a meaning postulate can be supplied that, in conjunction with postulates for the strong domain and complete awareness hypotheses, would yield strong exhaustiveness.

This would account for the validity of the following argument (suggested by an example due to Ede Zimmermann (p.c.)):

<u>All parents know which of their children have been innoculated.</u>
All parents know which of their children have not been innoculated.

I refrain, however, from formulating the requisite postulates.

9. The issue being raised here for my analysis, and essentially the response to it I will propose, were brought to my attention by Angelika Kratzer.

10. It is not just having false beliefs that can induce this; merely being uncertain suffices. Thus, consider the following scenario that G&S offer as intuitive support for strong exhaustiveness (1984, 87):

> Suppose that John knows of everyone who walks that he/she does; that of no one who doesn't walk, he believes that he/she does; but that of some individual that actually does not walk, he doubts whether he/she walks or not. In such a situation, John would not say of himself that he knows who walks. We see no reason to override his judgement and claim that in this situation, John does know who walks. This seems to suggest that for John to know who walks, he should not only know of everyone who walks that he/she does, but also of everyone who doesn't that he/she doesn't.

Again, it seems to me that the appropriate conclusion is that John knows who walks but he doesn't know that he knows this. (Notice, incidentally, that this scenario employs the complete awareness hypothesis, as is clear from the condition of doubting--if John were not aware of the existence of certain individuals who don't walk (in the relevant domain), he obviously couldn't be in doubt as to whether or not they walk.)

This line of reasoning will also, I think, handle a similar objection raised by Tomas Vlk (Barbara Partee, p.c.) to the effect that, if John knows of three of four people who left that they left, but he is unaware of the existence of the fourth person, then the sentence *John mostly knows which people left.* is false. I would argue, again, that it is true, but that we cannot infer from it that John knows that he knows which people left.

11. Boër (1978, 319) denies this, claiming that for, *e.g.*, *John stole the cheese* to be true, John "would have to identify as cheese-thieves all AND ONLY genuine cheese-thieves." But Boër, like G&S, does not consider the objective point of view I have been arguing for.

12. Angelika Kratzer has noted (p.c.) that the implicature excluding false information appears in other linguistic contexts too, for example, on a multiple-choice test with the instruction: "Circle the correct answers." The clever student who turns in the test with all answers, thus all correct answers, circled, should not expect a good grade.

V

A Nonquantificational Analysis of *Wh*-Phrases, II: Asymmetries Between *Wh*-Phrases and Indefinites

1 Introduction

The analysis in chapter III is predicated on the numerous parallels in quantificational behavior between *wh*-phrases and indefinite NPs, the behavior of the latter type of phrase being the original motivation for the LHK theory. The parallels extend as well to the evidence upon which I proposed a general (partial) derivation of the restrictive term of the quantifier: that it contains the presuppositions of the nuclear scope. Despite these similarities, there are also differences in the distribution of the quantifiability of *wh*-phrases and indefinites, and it is the purpose of this chapter to investigate these differences and extend the analysis developed in chapter III, in order to account for them. In section 2 I present the data illustrating the asymmetrical behavior, and arrive at a generalization about it. Section 3 is an attempt to put some theoretical teeth into this generalization: I argue that the asymmetry results from the syntactic displacement of *wh*-phrases due to the process of *wh*-movement, which has an effect on the logical representation of sentences containing *wh*-phrases. My account is couched within certain assumptions concerning the relation between the syntactic structure of these sentences and their logical representation; and in particular, I propose that these two representations are mediated by a third—Logical Form. I give a number of arguments suggestive of the utility (if not the necessity) of appealing to this level of representation, ranging from the effect of presupposition accommodation (section 3.3) to the behavior of *wh*-phrases in Japanese (section

103

3.4.1) and in multiple-*wh*-constructions (section 3.4.2). Having established the conditions under which *wh*-phrases are not quantifiable, I finally, in section 4, turn to an account of the interpretation and logical representation of these *wh*-clauses.

2 Data and Generalizations

We saw in section 3.1 of chapter III how the quantifiability of *wh*-phrases in complement clauses is parallelled by the quantifiability of indefinites in adjunct *if*-clauses; this is again illustrated by the sentences in (105), which can both have the interpretation paraphrased in (106):

(105) a. The maître d' seldom knows which patrons of Maxim's are rich.
b. If a patron of Maxim's is rich, the maître d' seldom knows it.
(106) Few patrons of Maxim's who are rich are such that the maître d' knows of them that they are rich.

This symmetry breaks down, however, when the structural relation between the quantifier (adverb of quantification) and the phrase to be quantified (*wh*-phrase or indefinite) is changed; this is illustrated by the following sentences:

(107) a. The maître d' knows which patrons of Maxim's are seldom rich.
b. If a patron of Maxim's is seldom rich, the maître d' knows it.

In contrast to (105.a), in (107.a) the *wh*-phrase cannot be understood as quantified by the adverb, and the latter only has a frequency interpretation (in the sentences in (105), the adverb might also be understood as a frequency quantifier, though this is unlikely with a verb such as *know*). But the indefinite in (107.b) can be quantified by the adverb. That is, the sentences in (107) may have the following respective paraphrases:

(108) a.   For all patrons of Maxim's for whom the times when they
            are rich are few, the maître d' knows of them that the times
            when they are rich are few.
       b.   For all times when few patrons of Maxim's are (such that
            they are) rich, the maître d' knows this.

In fact, (107.b) can also have the interpretation in (108.a), in which the
adverb serves as a frequency quantifier; however, the usual pragmatic
incompatibility of a frequency quantification with a predicate such as
rich (just as with *know*, as noted parenthetically above) makes this
reading less salient, and also accounts for the pragmatic oddness of
(107.a). The real contrast is in the lack of the interpretation in (108.b)
for the sentence in (107.a).
      The only difference between the sentences in (105) and those in
(107) is in the position of the adverb of quantification: in the latter it is
in the matrix clause, in the former in the embedded clause. Consider in
this light the following sentences:

(109) a.   Which patrons of Maxim's are seldom rich?
       b.   A patron of Maxim's is seldom rich.

While (109.b) is ambiguous between the reading where the indefinite is
quantified by the adverb, with the sentence meaning that few patrons of
Maxim's are rich, and the (pragamtically odd) frequency reading of the
adverb, in which case the indefinite has default universal or generic
force (unless it is a specific, *i.e.* widescope, indefinite), the question in
(109.a) only has the frequency reading, and the *wh*-phrase is not associated with any particular quantificational force. That is, the question
is not asking for a list of (the identities of) few patrons of Maxim's
who are rich, but for a list of any patrons of Maxim's for whom the
times when they are rich are few. This recalls the examples in chapter
III, section 4.1, in which the *wh*-clause is not presupposed by the matrix complement, and the *wh*-phrase is not quantified; the following
sentence also illustrates this:

(110) The maître d' seldom wonders which patrons of Maxim's are
       rich.

The generalization suggested by the data in (105), (107), and (109) is that *wh*-phrases cannot be quantified by a same-clause adverb of quantification, but only by one in a higher clause, while indefinites can be quantified by an adverb of quantification in either the same clause or in a higher one.

Another asymmetry between *wh*-phrases and indefinites is that the latter display a kind of quantificational ambiguity, in certain circumstances, that the former fail to. The following sentence illustrates this ambiguity (pointed out by Milsark (1974); see also Carlson (1977)):

(111) Rich people often eat at Maxim's.

On one reading, (111) means that many rich people eat at Maxim's (habitually), that is, the adverb is quantifying the indefinite. On the other reading it means that the times when there are rich people eating at Maxim's are many; here the adverb is a frequency quantifier, and the indefinite has existential force.[1] In contrast, *wh*-questions do not display this ambiguity:

(112) Which people often eat at Maxim's?

This can only ask about the set of people who eat at Maxim's on many occasions, *i.e.* the adverb is only a frequency quantifier, just like in (109.a).

The ambiguity with indefinites survives embedding in an *if*-clause:

(113) If rich people often eat at Maxim's, the maître d' knows it.

In fact, there is a threefold ambiguity here: the indefinite may either have existential force, the force of the embedded adverb of quantification, or the force of a quantifier in the matrix clause, the implicit universal. The latter type of reading is easier to get with an explicit adverb:

(114) If rich people often eat at Maxim's, the maître d' seldom knows it.

Since *know* is like *rich* in pragmatically disfavoring a frequency interpretation of the adverb, the most salient reading of this sentence is where *seldom* quantifies over *rich people* and *often* has a frequency intepretation. Such multiple ambiguity contrasts with the univocity displayed in embedded wh-clauses:

(115) The maître d' seldom knows which people often eat at Maxim's.

The wh-phrase here has neither existential force nor the force of the embedded adverb, but the force of the matrix adverb of quantification.

    The ambiguity of the indefinites in (111) and (113)-(114) has a natural and straightforward account in terms of the LHK theory, as shown independently by Wilkinson (1986; 1991) and Gerstner and Krifka (1987): the interpretation of the indefinite is a function of which argument of the quantifier it resides in in the logical translation. Specifically, if the indefinite is in the restrictive term of the quantifier it gets quantified by the latter, while if it is in the nuclear scope it gets existentially evaluated (recall the truth definition (10) in chapter I, which requires there to be some satisfying assignment for the nuclear scope, thus in effect stipulating its existential closure). In the latter case, the adverb has a frequency interpretation. For the sentence in (111), the two readings are rendered by the following translations (where the frequency intepretation is (far too simplistically, but for present purposes adequately) represented, as in chapter III, section 3.2 (34), by using a sortal predicate over temporal intervals in the restrictive term):

(116) a.   MANY [rich-person$'(x)$] [eat-at-Maxim's$'(x)$]
     b.   MANY [TIME(t)] [rich-person$'(x)$ & eat-at-Maxim's$'(x,t)$]

The difference between indefinites and wh-phrases suggested by the data in (111)-(115), then, is that the latter, unlike the former, do not have the option of being in the nuclear scope.

    Both this difference as well as the asymmetry in wh-phrase quantifiability seen in the (a)-sentences in (105), (107), and (109), as against the fully symmetrical quantifiability of the indefinites in the corresponding (b)-sentences, are straightforwardly accounted for by assuming that wh-phrases always take wide scope with respect to a same-clause quantifier.[2] If this is so, it would be enlightening to correlate this logical property with some grammatical property. I would like

to suggest that *wh*-movement is such a property. The idea is that it is
the structural representation resulting from *wh*-movement that the kind
of logical representation I have presented in chapter III derives from;
and in this structural representation the *wh*-phrases are no longer in the
scope of the same-clause quantifier, therefore in the logical representation they are neither in its restrictive term, nor a fortiori in its nuclear
scope. The justifiability of this idea is examined in the next section.

3 *Wh*-Movement as a Determinant of *Wh*-Phrase Quantifiability

I acknowledge right off the bat that I will not prove that *wh*-
movement is the reason why *wh*-phrases have wide scope. This is
because both my evidence and my arguments concern essentially logicosemantic properties of *wh*-phrases, whereas *wh*-movement is essentially a syntactic process, since it manipulates syntactic constituent structure. The issue at hand is the question of whether there is a syntactic
level of representation, distinct from the surface syntactic structure (S-
structure), that feeds semantic intepretation; in other words, the question of whether there is a level of Logical Form (LF), distinct from a
purely logical representation, such as I have used throughout this
study. Because LF is hypothesized as a syntactic level of representation, evidence for it must be syntactic in nature; as Pesetsky (1987,
121) puts it, "what is paramount in exploring Logical Form are [*sic*]
its properties as a syntactic level on the road to interpretation, not one
or another arbitrarily assigned semantic property like disambiguation of
scope." The properties I am investigating are precisely the latter, and
there are certainly nonsyntactic ways of treating them. It is for this
reason that my arguments and evidence do not in and of themselves
show that the wide-scope property of *wh*-phrases is due to *wh*-move-
ment.

Nevertheless, I will continue to present my case in terms of *wh*-
movement, for the following reasons. For one thing, there is in some
cases undeniably a correlation between the syntactic movement of a
wh-phrase and its widescope interpretation (section 3.2). Secondly,
certain interesting consequences result from combining this assumption
with that of taking the effect of (one type of) presupposition accommodation to be represented syntactically (*i.e.*, at LF) (section 3.3). Third,

my arguments can be seen as providing independent semantic support for the claim of LF wh-movement in cases where there is clearly no syntactic movement, as in languages like Japanese (section 3.4.1) and in multiple wh-constructons in English (section 3.4.2), although admittedly this evidence only has force insofar as the strictly syntactic evidence for LF wh-movement that has been adduced in these cases is accepted. There is also a reason of a different nature, bound up with my conception of the logicosemantic character of wh-phrases: I have argued that wh-phrases, like indefinites, are logically treated as open sentences, and if this is so, then there is no logical or semantic reason why one type of phrase but not the other should have different scope properties-- indeed, from a strictly logicosemantic point of view, there is just one type of phrase; but from a syntactic point of view there are clearly two types of phrases. Moreover, the most common nonsyntactic ways of assigning scope, namely, quantifying in and quantifier storage (though the former is in a sense syntactic too), are specifically operations on quantifiers, and this is incompatible with my treatment of wh-phrases (the same is of course true of the LHK treatment of indefinites). For all these reasons, in short, appealing to wh-movement (and to LF) to explain a logical property of wh-phrases, while not strictly necessary, seems nevertheless not entirely without some positive motivation.

3.1 Syntactic Assumptions and the Mapping to Logical Form

In order to show the effect of wh-movement at LF, I need to be precise about certain mappings from S-structure to LF, obviously that of wh-movement, but also that of adverbs of quantification. In addition, in light of the LHK theory, the LF representation of the nuclear scope and restrictive term needs to be specified, that is, how these logico-semantic functions are read off of LF. For the first two I will rely on longstanding treatments; for the last, I draw upon recent work of Molly Diesing.

It is quite uncontroversial that adverbs of quantification have sentential scope; this is the position of Lewis (1975) and Heim (1982), for instance: this seems to be the minimal requirement, since, as we have seen, such adverbs can quantify over all arguments of a predicate. A standard way to represent this scope in LF is to adjoin the quantifier to the sentence node (*cf.* Heim (1982, 133*ff.*) and the rule of Quantifier Raising (QR) in May (1977)). This results in the following type of structure (where Ω represents a quantifier):

(117)

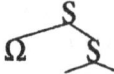

In this structure, Ω is a potential binder of any free variable dominated by (the lower) S. In accordance with the LHK theory, I want next to consider how S is to be divided into the restrictive term and the nuclear scope of Ω. (I will continue to speak this way, though it should be clear that what is meant is the division of the syntactic structure into parts which translate in the logical representation as the restrictive term and nuclear scope.)

Heim (1982) produced the restrictive term also by adjunction to S, within the scope of the quantifier, of course (which was stipulated to adjoin as a leftmost constituent. This adjunction is assumed as the S-structure representation for *if*-clauses, but for NPs, it occurs as an LF operation, and leaves behind a coindexed trace, which translates as a free variable. The nuclear scope consists of the tree structure dominated by the S-node to which the restrictive term and quantifier have been adjoined; (118) illustrates this LF, in which the restrictive term is an NP:

(118)

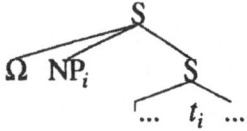

While this characterization of the quantificational logical form is semantically perfectly adequate, it is less closely tied to the syntactic representation than might be hoped for in an LF, which is, after all, supposed to be a syntactic level of representation. Recently, Diesing (1990b) has made a case for a closer correspondence between the syntax and the logical form. Her proposal starts from the assumption that there are two possible subject positions in S-structure, an idea that has been argued for on a number of independent syntactic grounds (*cf.* Kitagawa (1986), Kuroda (1988), Sportiche (1988), Diesing (1990a)). Diesing implements her analysis in terms of the phrase structure theory of Chomsky (1986), according to which the sentential domain is taken to be a projection (in the sense of X-bar theory) of Inflection, dominated by the IP node (corresponding to S in earlier theories). One possible subject position is the daughter of IP, [Spec,IP][3]; this corresponds to the standard subject position of earlier theories. The other potential subject position is within the VP, in [Spec,VP]. The partial tree structure in (119) illustrates these assumptions:

(119)

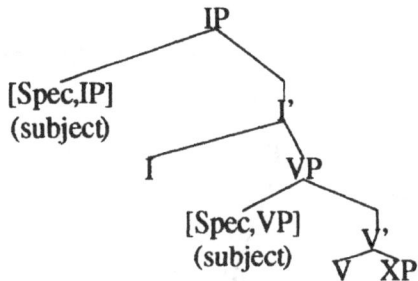

Whether a subject occupies [Spec,IP] or [Spec,VP] in S-structure depends both on the language and on properties of particular sentences: *e.g.* in English it is claimed that the subject is always in [Spec,IP] in S-structure, while in German it can be in either [Spec,IP] or [Spec,VP]; see Diesing for details. What is of interest for my purposes is the relation of these positions to LF.

   Concering this, Diesing observed that the structure in (119) affords a transparent account of the ambiguity exhibited by sentences such as (111) if it is assumed that a subject may occupy either [Spec,IP] or [Spec,VP] at LF and that these positions in the syntax become part of the restrictive term and the nuclear scope, respectively, in the logical representation. To implement this, Diesing proposes a mapping hypothesis, according to which the LF representation of the VP-subtree in (119) maps to the nuclear scope, while that of the superordinate structure, which Diesing calls the IP-level structure, maps to the restrictive term (the IP-level structure must, of course,

exclude the IP-adjoined quantifier itself). As an illustration, partial LFs
for the two readings of the sentence in (111) are given in (120).

(120) a.

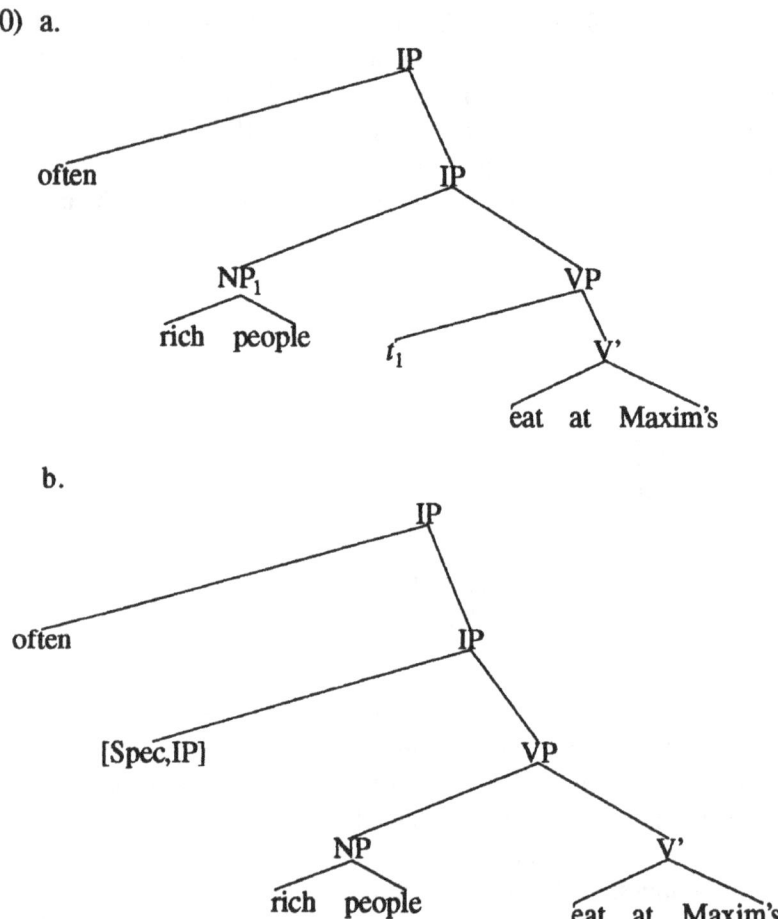

b.

Given Diesing's mapping hypothesis, there is a straightforward relation
between these LFs and the logical translations in (116) (at least with
respect to the lexical arguments; the temporal variables might have to
be handled differently). The indefinite NPs translate as open sentences,
containing a free variable; the NP-trace translates as an occurrence of
the same variable as the NP. In (120.a), since the subject in [Spec,IP]
maps to the restrictive term, it gets quantified by the adverb. Note that
the trace in [Spec,VP], although in the nuclear scope, will not get

existential force according to the evaluation algorithm (10) of chapter I, because the assignment g'', which is the source of the existential closure of the nuclear scope, differs from g' only on new variables; therefore the variable translating the trace will get evaluated by g', which depends on the quantifier. In (120.b), with the subject in [Spec,VP], in the nuclear scope, it does not get quantified by the adverb, but receives existential force from g''.[4]

3.2 *The Effect of* Wh-*movement*

Having presented an account of LF that mirrors the LHK restricted quantification structure, let us now return to the effect of *wh*-movement. The standard position regarding the syntactic operation (at least since Bresnan (1972)) is that, subsequent to this transformation,[5] the *wh*-phrase is in a position outside of the sentence node, though still part of the clausal structure. To be specific, in terms of the phrase structure theory used above, superordinate to IP is the complementizer projection, dominated by CP and it is to the [Spec,CP] that *wh*-phrases are claimed to move, leaving behind a coindexed trace. This is illustrated by the following partial LF tree structure:

(121)

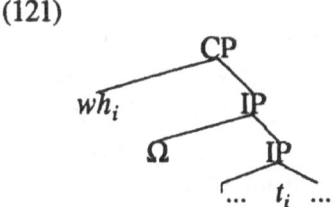

As this structure clearly shows, the *wh*-phrase is not within the scope of the quantifier subsequent to *wh*-movement. This means that, when this structure is translated into the logical representation, with the *wh*-phrase being an open sentence, the free variable it contains will not be bound by the quantifier; and since the trace of the *wh*-phrase translates as the same variable, it will not get bound either, or get existentially evaluated, since it is not a new variable. This accounts for the absence of *wh*-phrase quantification by a same-clause quantifier, as well for the impossibility of a *wh*-phrase getting bound within the nuclear scope of its clause.

When the *wh*-phrase is in an embedded clause, however, it is within the scope of a matrix IP-adjoined quantifier, as the following structure illustrates:

(122)

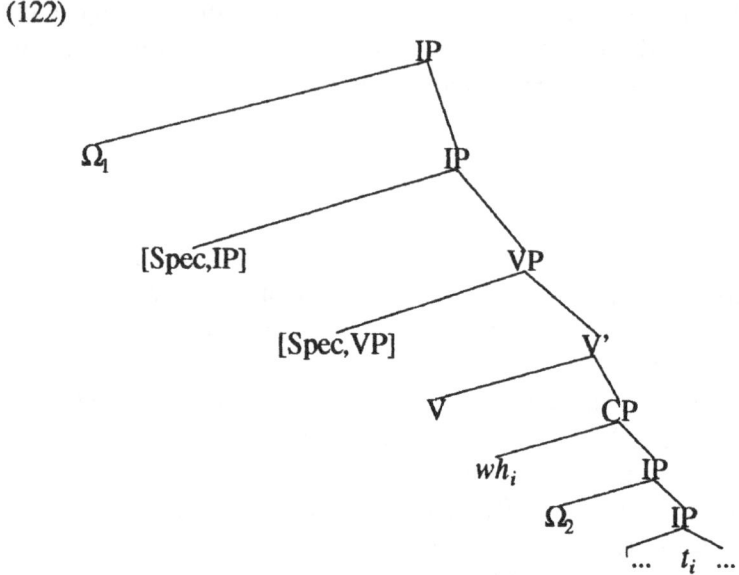

Thus, although, the *wh*-phrase cannot get bound by Ω_2, it can get bound by Ω_1—or can it? As (122) also shows, the *wh*-phrase is within the matrix nuclear scope, therefore, according to Diesing's mapping hypothesis, it should be bound within it, getting an existential interpretation. But, as we have seen, such an interpretation does not occur. What, then, prevents the *wh*-phrase from being bound within the matrix nuclear scope? The answer is presupposition accommodation. As we have seen in chapter III, section 4.2, when the matrix verb in a quantified structure such as (122) presupposes its complement, this is a presupposition of the nuclear scope, and consequently becomes a part of the restrictive term of the matrix quantifier, which therefore binds the free variable in the translation of the *wh*-phrase. (I return in section 4 to cases where the *wh*-complement is not presupposed.) This means that the variable in the translation of the occurrence of the *wh*-phrase that is in the complement clause, although within the matrix nuclear scope, is not new there, hence will be ignored by the assignment function that evaluates this clause, according to (10) from chapter I.

This raises a question: does presupposition accommodation affect LF, or is it only in the logical translation that its effect is manifested? I consider this question in the next subsection, but first, I want to note one additional consequence of the effect of *wh*-movement on *wh*-phrase quantifiability.

In light of this account, it is interesting to consider what happens in sentences in which the the *wh*-phrase has moved out of its own clause, as in the following examples:

(123) a. Which patrons of Maxim's does the maître d' seldom know are rich?
   b. Which students does the principal usually discover cheat on the final exam?
   c. Which gifts does Mary mostly remember that she got for her birthday last year?
   d. Which colleagues does Bill often acknowledge that he gets a good idea from?

The *wh*-phrases in these sentences cannot be understood to have the quantificational force of the adverb, even though the latter is in the matrix clause and the *wh*-phrase comes from the embedded clause; instead, the interpretations are analogous to that of (109.a), with the adverb having only a frequency reading. And the reason for this, I suggest, is just the same: subsequent to *wh*-movement, the *wh*-phrase occupies the matrix [Spec,CP], hence is outside of the scope of the matrix adverb, *i.e.* the configuration is exactly as in (121). If, on the other hand, the sentences in (123) are in turn embedded under a predicate that presupposes them, the *wh*-phrase will be quantified by an adverb in the new matrix clause, as exemplified by the following sentence:

(124) John mostly found out which patrons of Maxim's the maître d' seldom knows are rich.

The upshot of this is that, as long as there is a quantifier in a higher clause than the *wh*-phrase, the latter can be quantified by it, by being accommodated into its restrictive term; but if the quantifier and *wh*-phrase are in the same clause, even if this arises from *wh*-movement, then the *wh*-phrase cannot be quantified by the adverb; and the reason, I have argued, is that, subsequent to *wh*-movement, the *wh*-phrase is not within the scope of the same-clause quantifier.

3.3 *Presupposition Accommodation and LF*

The effect of presupposition accommodation, i.e, that the embedded *wh*-clause becomes part of the restrictive term of the matrix quantifier, can certainly be represented in an LF tree structure; for example, subsequent to accommodation, the structure in (122) might take the following form:

(125)

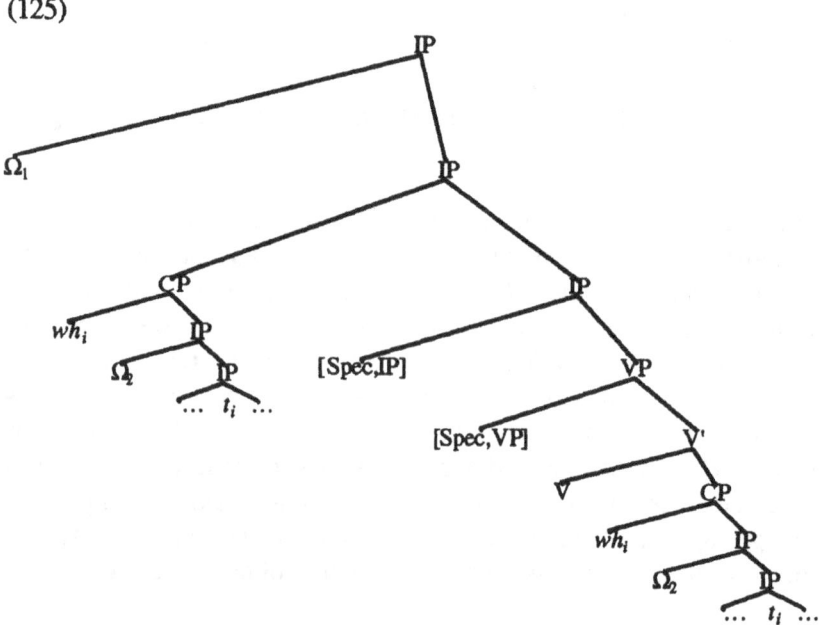

This structure exactly reflects the final logical representation that renders the correct interpretation of sentences in which the *wh*-phrase is quantified, and in this respect is consistent with my use of LF to mediate between S-structure and the logical translation. There is, however, a serious question concerning the derivation of a structure such as (125). In particular, note that there are two matrix IP-adjunctions here, and they must occur in such a way that only the structural relation indicated obtains; if the adjunction that renders the effect of presupposition accommodation were to the structure to which the quantifier were already adjoined—resulting in the structure in (126)—the wrong interpretation would result.

(126)

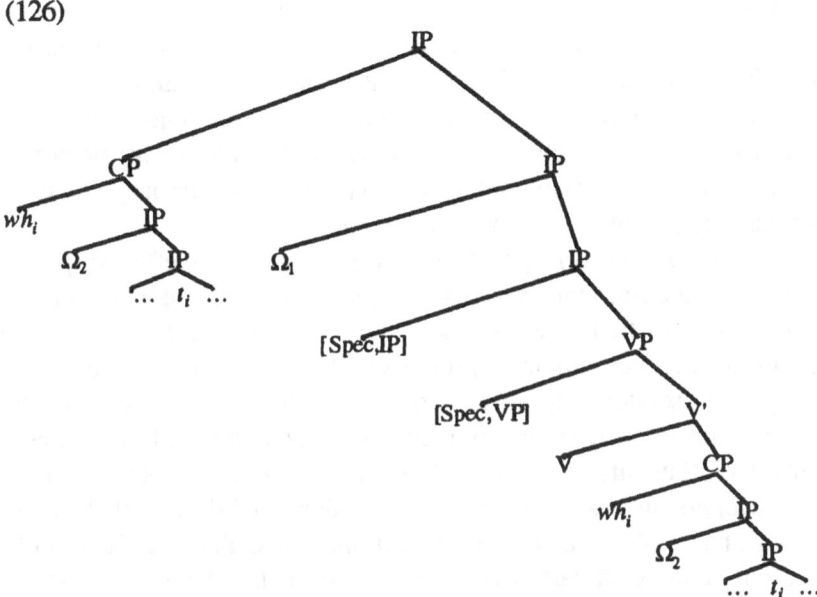

In interpreting this structure, the variable in the translation of the *wh*-phrase would remain free, thus have to get its values from the context; and I see no a priori grounds for excluding this possibility. It might be thought that (126) is excluded as a violation of the prohibition against vacuous quantification (*cf.* chapter I (11)), since it seems that Ω_1 does not bind a variable in its restrictive term. But the matrix [Spec,IP] position is in its restrictive term, and it is certainly possible for that to contain a phrase that translates as a free variable, as in the following sentence:

(127) A farmer usually knows which crops bring a good price.

If this sentence were interpreted in accordance with (126), it should mean that for some contextually supplied set of crops that bring the best prices, most farmers are such that they know that these crops bring a good price. But (127) cannot mean that; rather, it means that for most pairs of a farmer and a crop that brings a good price, the farmer knows that the crop brings a good price—in accordance with the structure in (125).6

In short, although (126) must be ruled out, apparently it won't be on semantic grounds. I do not, however, see any motivated syntactic means of excluding it, while allowing (125). One can always stipulate that presupposition accommodation precedes QR in the derivation of LF, though I know of no independent reason for assuming this. (My rendering the effect of accommodation as Chomsky-adjunction is also not crucial—I use it because that is standard in the theory of phrase-structure I am employing; an adjunction that created ternary branching would face the same problem of motivation.)

Another potential problem with representing the effect of presupposition accommodation at LF concerns the issue of whether it is appropriate to treat this as a sentential process at all, on a par, for example, are the syntactic processes of *wh*-movement and QR. In chapter III, section 4.3, I discussed presupposition accommodation as a general discourse process, not confined to the domain of the sentence. However, there are, as I alluded to in note 16 of that chapter, two kinds of presupposition accommodation in the theory of Heim (1983b), local and global, and this distinction is, I think, especially significant in the present context. In particular, it is only through local accommodation that the presuppositions of the nuclear scope become part of the restrictive term of a quantifier. And it appears that local accommodation lives up to its name, in that it is evidently subject to fairly severe locality restrictions; specifically, the accommodation must be to the restrictive term of the next highest quantifier in the tree (*i.e.*, the closest c-commanding quantifier). Consider, for example, the following sentence:

(128) John is seldom surprised that a farmer usually knows which crops bring a good price.

The *wh*-phrase *which crops* can only have the force of the adverb *usually*, not that of *seldom*. Again, since the indefinite *a farmer* is also in the restrictive term of *usually*, it is not the prohibition against vacuous quantification that prevents the *wh*-phrase from going into the matrix clause. Instead, it seems that the domain of local accommodation for the *wh*-phrase itself prevents this.7 In contrast, global accommodation is manifestly not bounded in this way, as the following sentence illustrates:

(129) John knows that Mary thinks that Sue likes his brother.

Taking *his* to refer to John, this entire sentence presupposes that John has a brother—this is a typical effect of global accommodation. (I return to global accommodation, in particular of definites, as in (129), in appendix B.) But, as noted in chapter III, section 4.3, the presuppositions of the nuclear scope, which are locally accommodated into the restrictive term, do not necessarily survive as presuppositions of the sentence as a whole. This is expected, since they are confined to the domain of the next highest quantifier, thus do not reach the discourse level. What all this suggests is that local accommodation may indeed be a kind of syntactic process, since it is subject to a syntactically determinable locality constraint. And if it is a syntactic process, then it is possibly an LF operation.

It seems, then, that it may indeed be appropriate to represent local (though less plausibly global) presupposition accommodation at LF. I would now like to suggest that, if this is the case, it allows an interesting account of the difference, noted in chapter III, section 3.3, between the logical translations of *wh*-complement clauses (*i.e.* indirect questions) and free relatives. Recall that, unlike the former, the translation of the free relative appears only in the restrictive term, while in the nuclear scope remains only an individual variable; thus, the translation of *Mary seldom likes who she meets.* is (130.a), not (130.b):

(130) a.   FEW[PERSON(x) & meet'(m,x)][like'(m,x)]
       b.   FEW[PERSON(x) & meet'(m,x)][like'(m,[PERSON(x) & meet'(m,x)])]

Obviously, the problem with (130.b) is that *like* does not take a proposition-denoting complement (that is, something that denotes a proposition when a value is supplied to the free variable), but an individual-denoting complement, as in (130.a); in other words, (130.b) violates the selectional restrictions of the predicate. If the effect of (local) accommodation is represented at LF, we can use this lexicosemantic fact to distinguish between indirect questions and free relatives in the following way (I follow here ideas in Portner (1990), who proposes to distin-

guish gerunds from indirect questions (as I analyse them) along these
lines, and notes the utility of this for free relatives; though the particular implementation is mine). Let us take the S-structure of the sentence to be as in (131), which has, I think, substantial support in the
literature (the structural position of the adverb is not crucial):

(131)

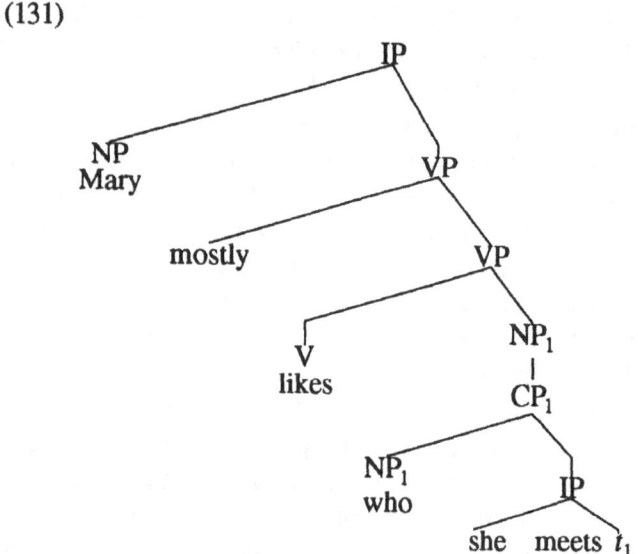

In other words, *like* subcategorizes for an NP, but this NP has the
internal structure of a CP—a proposition-denoting category. I have
assumed that the referential index of the *wh*-phrase percolates up to the
CP node, and thence to the immediately dominating NP; this seems
entirely reasonable on semantic grounds. Now, when this structure is
transformed into an LF, the result must be semantically licit. The
question here is, what is the effect of presupposition accommodation of
the free relative?[8] If the CP were simply copied into it LF position,
with a copy thus remaining in the complement position of *like*, we
would end up with the translation (130.b), which, as noted, violates the
verb's selectional requirements. But there is another possibility: instead
of being copied, the CP may actually be moved, leaving only a trace
behind. Moreover, given the structure in (131), that trace will be of the
category NP, thus of the appropriate (indeed, necessary) semantic type.
The resulting LF, on this account, is the following structure:

(132)

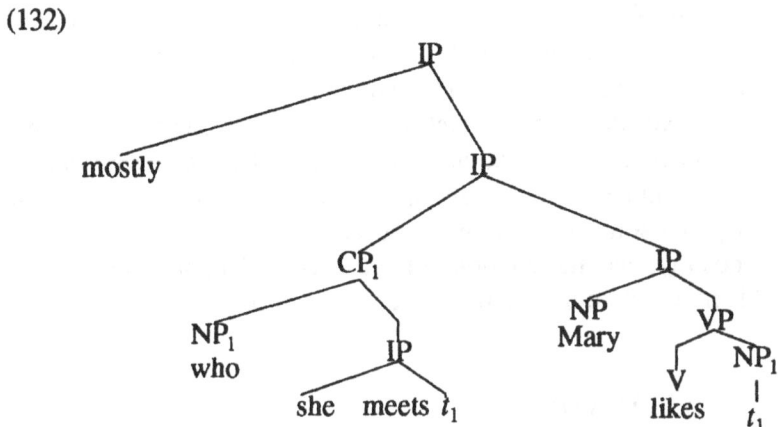

Since the NP-complement bears the same index as the *wh*-phrase, thus will translate as an occurrence of the same variable, this structure yields the correct translation in (130.a). In short, it is the clash between the selectional requirements of the matrix predicate and the clausal semantics of free relatives that forces the latter, when accommodated, to move rather than be copied. This clash is nicely resolved in terms of an LF representation such as (132), deriving from the S-structure (131), because the NP category, which is subcategorized for and selected by the matrix predicate, bears the trace of the free relative, thus yielding the required translation. (This is not to deny that such a distinction could not be made without reference to LF, just that this level of representation is a natural one at which to express it, since it combines syntactic and semantic information.)[9]

To summarize this section, I have shown what effects presupposition accommodation would have if it is taken to be represented at LF. In the first place, it seems that it is only (or most plausibly) local accommodation that is an LF operation, in view of its strict locality, which makes it plausible to treat as a syntactic process. Even so, local accommodation can have two distinct implementations: either copying (as with indirect questions) or moving (as with free relatives). We may assume that copying is the default (though this is admittedly not typical of syntactic operations), while moving is induced on semantic grounds by type-incompatibility with selectional properties of the predicate involved. This accounts for the difference between indirect questions and free relatives: with the latter movement is required to avoid just such incompatibility, while with the former there is no clash, thus copying suffices.[10] There remain unresolved issues, such as just how to exclude structures such as (126), and whether the transformational effect of accommodation results from independent grammatical processes or must be separately stipulated; but the discussion in this section gives some indication of the consequences of taking (local) presupposition accommodation to have effect at LF, and these suggest that this may not be an inappropriate thing to do.[11]

3.4 LF Wh-*Movement*

While I have been arguing throughout this section for a scope effect of *wh*-movement, all the examples I have discussed so far involve only *wh*-movement that happens in any case in the syntax. In this subsection, I present evidence that the scope effect of *wh*-movement is realized even when there is clearly no *wh*-movement in the syntax. The conclusion I would like to draw from this is that *wh*-movement must also occur at LF, in order for the required scope relations to arise. Again, this conclusion must be tempered with the recognition, acknowledged at the beginning of this section, that the empirical fact of wide scope can be accounted for by other analytical means than *wh*-movement. Thus, to the extent that the facts I will cite are amenable to an account in terms of *wh*-movement, they should be seen as supporting independently motivated syntactic arguments for LF *wh*-movement (of which the previous subsection might also qualify as an instance).

The evidence I cite, concerning *wh*-constructions in languages that have no syntactic *wh*-movement and multiple-*wh*-constructions, is meant to be suggestive; obviously, more empirical work is needed to ascertain the validity of the evidence. It so happens that there is already a substantial literature in support of LF *wh*-movement for both these cases. For the first, the basic reference is Huang (1982a; 1982b); *cf.* also Lasnik and Saito (1984) and Nishigauchi (1986; 1990). For the second, standard references are Chomsky (1973) and Aoun, Hornstein, and Sportiche (1981); and more recently Pesetsky (1987). Pesetsky concludes that only some *wh*-phrases move at LF, a position at odds with what I will argue; I examine his case in section 3.4.3.

3.4.1 Japanese

Japanese is a language in which *wh*-phrases remain in the usual argument positions in the surface string, *i.e.*, they do not undergo *wh*-movement. Nevertheless, *wh*-phrases in Japanese display quantificational behavior that in many respects precisely parallels that found in English. That *wh*-phrases in Japanese exhibit quantificational variability was already pointed out by Nishigauchi (1986; 1990) (*cf.* chapter III, note 2); it turns out, moreover, that this quantifiability observes the same restriction indicated for English by the interpretive difference between sentences in (105.a) and (107.a). The following sentences are from Kawasaki (1990):

(133) a. John-wa taitei [dare-ga ukar-u-ka] shit-te i-ru
         TOP mostly who-NOM pass-PRES-Q know PRES
         'John mostly knows who will pass'
     b. John-wa [dare-ga taitei ukar-u-ka] shit-te i-ru
         'John knows who usually passes'

These sentences have the same interpretations as the corresponding English sentences, that is, the *wh*-phrase is quantified by the adverb in (133.a), which is about most people who will pass; while in (133.b) the *wh*-phrase is not quantified by the adverb, which only has a frequency interpretation. Kawasaki gives evidence that *taitei*, like its English counterpart, has IP as its scope (*i.e.* sentential scope). Therefore, in view of the lack of quantifiability in (133.b), she concludes that the *wh*-word *dare* moves to [Spec,CP] in LF, where it is outside the scope of the quantifier.

3.4.2 Multiple-wh-constructions

The quantificational behavior of *wh*-phrases in multiple-*wh*-constructions also argues for LF *wh*-movement. We have already seen examples of these constructions, in which all the *wh*-phrases are quantified by a single adverb of quantification; the following is another example:

(134) The valet seldom knows which patrons own which cars.

This means that for few pairs of a patron and a car the patron owns does the valet know that the patron owns the car. If the adverb is in the embedded clause, in contrast, neither of the *wh*-phrases is quantified by it:

(135) The valet knows which patrons seldom own which cars.

This means that for all pairs of a patron and a car such that the times when the patron owns the car are few, the valet knows that the patron owns the car and that the times when this relation holds are few; that is, the adverb has a frequency interpretation and the *wh*-phrases receive universal force (from the matrix implicit universal quantifier). The difference between (134) and (135) is exactly the same pattern displayed in (105.a) and (107.a), and suggests to me the same account: both (and, in general, all) *wh*-phrases move to [Spec,CP], where they are beyond the scope of and hence not quantifiable by the adverb of quantification. Moreover, since on the surface there is only one *wh*-phrase already in that position, sentences such as (135) clearly show that some *wh*-movement must occur at LF; in the case of *wh-in-situ*, English is thus similar to Japanese.

3.4.3 *Do All* Wh-*phrases Move at LF?*

This argument for LF *wh*-movement partly contradicts the conclusions of Pesetsky (1987). Pesetsky also appeals to multiple-*wh*-constructions to argue for LF *wh*-movement, but only in the case of what he calls non-D-linked *wh*-phrases, where D-linking (discourse-linking) is characterized in terms that indicate it means the same thing as pragmatic presupposition (*cf.* chapter III, section 4.2). So Pesetsky argues in effect that *wh*-phrases whose substitution-values are not pragmatically presupposed, not already part of the context of utterance, do move in LF; while *wh*-phrases whose substitution-values are pragmatically presupposed do not move in LF, but are bound by a Baker-style Q operator (*cf.* Baker (1970)). I will not go into the details of Pesetsky's argument, which is based on an attempt to account for acceptable violations of the Superiority Condition (Chomsky (1973)); his proposed dichotomy appears, however, to be incompatible with my account of the quantifiability facts. In particular, the *wh*-phrases in (135) should be able to qualify as D-linked, since it is quite conceivable that a given set of patrons and cars is part of the context. If this is so, then according to Pesetsky's account, they should not undergo LF *wh*-movement; but then they remain within the scope of the adverb of quantification at LF, and so should be quantified: since they are not, I conclude they must move beyond the scope of the quantifier, and this must happen at LF, if this is an effect of *wh*-movement.

Again, this conclusion has force only insofar as my account in terms of *wh*-movement is preferable to a purely semantic account, one that doesn't assume any logical contribution of *wh*-movement. Whereas, if Pesetsky is right, an indisputably syntactic effect (Superiority) is accounted by crucially assuming LF *wh*-movement to apply differentially.[12] In that case, my appeal to *wh*-movement cannot be correct, and the wide-scope property would have to derive from nonsyntactic means. However, Comorovski (1989) argues that Pesetsky's account of the Superiority facts is flawed, which, if so, would substantially weaken his case for restricting LF *wh*-movement.[13] Comorovski raises both theoretical and empirical problems for Pesetsky's account, which I will not try to evaluate here; I will just take note of one of the empirical problems.

Pesetsky proposes to subsume the Superiority Condition under a version of the Nested Dependency Condition, which he formulates as follows (p.105): "If two *wh*-trace dependencies overlap, one must contain the other." The following examples evidently contradict this, according to the usual structural analyses (the first example is from Comorovski (p.81(32))):

(136) a. Which crimes does the FBI know how to solve?
      b. Whose car is John trying to find out where to park?
      c. Which forms does Mary wonder when to turn in?

Comorovski points out that if the Nested Dependency Condition is construed as a processing constraint against ambiguous crossed dependencies (as in Fodor (1978)), then the relative acceptability (modulo the *wh*-island effect) of these sentences is accounted for, since the different categorial statuses of the *wh*-phrases (nominal *vs.* adverbial) eliminates ambiguity. But so construed, the utility of this constraint in explaining Superiority effects is doubtful, in view of sentences such as the following:

(137) a. *How did who solve the crimes?

    b.   *Where did who park the car?
    c.   *When did who turn in the forms?

These would be correctly ruled out on Pesetsky's analysis, because LF
wh-movement of the subject NP creates a crossed dependency. But if
the constraint is based on ambiguity, they should be acceptable, since
there is no doubt about how to resolve the dependencies. In view of the
absence of an account of the acceptability of the sentences in (136) on
Pesetsky's construal of the Nested Dependency Condition, the ungramma-
ticality of the sentences in (137) suggests that Superiority should not
be subsumed under it. But in that case, the argument for not moving
D-linked *wh*-phrases at LF, predicated on reducing Superiority violations to crossed dependencies, loses its force.

    Whether or not this argument against Pesetsky's analysis stands
up, it is worth pointing out that the essentially pragmatic distinction
he makes between *wh*-phrases with respect to undergoing LF *wh*-
movement has a number of consequences for the analysis of the semantics of these phrases. In particular, he proposes that non-D-linked *wh*-
phrases are in fact quantifiers, and this is why they move in LF; this
means that no distinction is being made between LF *wh*-movement and
a purely logical process such as Quantifier Raising, by which quantifiers take scope (Pesetsky is certainly not alone in making this equation). In contrast, D-linked *wh*-phrases are not analysed as quantifiers,
but—in analogy to Heim's treatment of indefinites—they are argued to
be unselectively bound by a question operator (though no explicit
semantic interpretation of this operator is given). This raises the question of how the variable quantifiability of *wh*-phrases—which obtains
with both the D-linked and the non-D-linked—would be accounted for,
a question to which I see no straightforward answer in terms of Pesetsky's analysis. It has nothing to do, for instance, with the question
operator, which is the Q morpheme of Baker (1970), since this is not a
quantifier. (I return to this in section 4, where I propose to use essentially Baker's operator in a restricted set of *wh*-contructions—precisely
those in which *wh*-phrases cannot be quantified.) Note, incidentally,
that I have no quarrel with Pesetsky's appeal to unselective binding—
indeed, I assume it too, in effect; the point, however, is that for Pesetsky, the unselectively bound *wh*-phrases remain *in situ*, whereas, on
my analysis, they must move to [Spec,CP].

In sum, then, I conclude that Pesetsky's analysis, according to which not all *wh*-phrases move at LF, is not proof against the opposite position, that all *wh*-phrases do move at LF, a position that, moreover, straightforwardly accounts for the facts I have discussed.

3.5 Summary

I have argued in this section that *wh*-movement is the core grammatical factor responsible for *wh*-phrases taking wide scope with respect to a same-clause quantifier: *wh*-movement results in an LF configuration in which the *wh*-phrase is outside the scope of a same-clause quantifier (this is also the position of May (1977) and Aoun, Hornstein, and Sportiche (1981) regarding the LF relationship between *wh*-phrases and quantifiers). This is the theoretical instantiation of the empirical generalization arrived at in section 2 above. My use of LF is not decisive, it must be acknowledged; but I have shown a number of interesting consequences that neatly follow from it: the interpretive difference between indirect questions and free relatives (assuming the effect of (local) presupposition accommodation is represented at LF); *wh*-phrase quantifiability in a languages such as Japanese, lacking syntactic *wh*-movement; and multiple-*wh*-phrase quantifiability.

It should perhaps be stressed at this point that what I have argued for is just that it is at the level of LF that *wh*-phrases must be in a position outside of the scope of a same-clause quantifier, here taken to be [Spec,CP]. It does not follow that this must also be the S-structure position of a *wh*-phrase which has undergone syntactic *wh*-movement (though I have also been assuming that it is). In fact, recently, it has been argued that in some languages the S-structure landing site of *wh*-movement is not [Spec,CP] but [Spec,IP]; *e.g.* in Yiddish (Diesing (1990a)) and Catalan (Bonet (1990)). I have not tested whether the behavior of *wh*-phrases with respect to quantification is the same in these languages as it is in English and Japanese, but if, as I would expect, it is, then clearly the *wh*-phrases cannot remain in [Spec,IP], since they would still be in the scope of an IP-adjoined quantifier, but must move to [Spec,CP] in LF, just like in English and Japanese (if my analysis is correct, of course). Nothing in Diesing's or Bonet's arguments excludes this, as they are only directed at surface syntactic phenomena, not interpretation, hence do not bear on LF. I therefore maintain that, as a general linguistic principle, *wh*-phrases move to [Spec,CP] in LF (or at least to some position beyond the scope of a sentential quantifier, but within the same clause).[14]

4   Nonquantifiable *Wh*-Phrases

I have been concerned throughout this study with accounting for the ability of *wh*-phrases to be quantified, and, in particular, to display variable quantificational force. In the course of my analysis, however, two kinds of syntactic environments have been encountered, in which *wh*-phrases are not quantified. One of these is a *wh*-clause embedded under a predicate that does not presuppose its complement, as discussed in chapter III, section 4.1 (*cf.* the examples in (42), (44)): because of this, according to my analysis, it does not get accommodated into the restrictive term of the matrix quantifier, and since being in this term is required for quantification, the *wh*-phrases cannot be quantified. The second environment of nonquantifiability is the matrix clause—in other words, a direct *wh*-question (*cf.* examples (109.a), (112) in section 2 above). Here, quantification is impossible because there is no higher clause and, as we have seen, *wh*-phrases always have wider scope than a same-clause quantifier. However, while my analysis so far accounts for the impossibility of *wh*-phrase quantification in these circumstances, it remains to account for the interpretation of the *wh*-clauses. Moreover, if nothing more is said, we have two problems: in the direct question, the *wh*-phrase is free, suggesting that it is evaluated solely from the context; while the embedded, nonpresupposed, *wh*-clause is within the nuclear scope of the matrix quantifier, which means that the *wh*-phrase should get an existential interpretation; but neither of these results is correct. In this section I will offer an account of the interpretation of these cases that avoids these difficulties.

To deal with such cases, I will essentially adopt Hamblin's (1973) analysis of questions. As we have seen in chapter II, section 4.1.1, Hamblin proposes to treat *wh*-phrases as denoting sets of possible individuals and, correspondingly, *wh*-clauses as denoting sets of possible propositions. This seems to me a perfectly reasonable approach when the *wh*-phrase is not otherwise associated with a quantificational force. It is on this point, in fact, that my analysis differs with Hamblin's, which treats *wh*-phrases always as sets of possible individuals, without regard to quantificational differences between them. In contrast, I want to restrict this treatment to those cases where a *wh*-phrase does not display quantificational variability.

In order to implement Hamblin's semantics within my representational approach, I adapt to my purposes a proposal going back to the analysis of questions by Katz and Postal (1964) and further developed by Baker (1970). Katz and Postal introduce an abstract morpheme Q, which they say (p.89) "indicates semantically... that the sentence is a question." Structures containing the Q morpheme are mostly matrix clauses, but in addition Katz and Postal assume that the complements of *wonder* and a few other verbs contain Q.[15] With all other *wh*-embedding verbs, the complement clause is not headed by Q (this differs from Baker's analysis; see below). What I want is for Q to head all matrix *wh*-clauses and also those *wh*-clauses that are complements of a predicate that does not presuppose its complement. For the former cases, we may simply stipulate that the matrix [Spec,CP] is inherently "[+Q]"—by this, I mean that the Q operator is always available for this position; this is analogous to the usual assumption regarding the syntactic admissibility of *wh*-phrases into this position (*i.e.*, that it is inherently "[+*wh*]"). For embedded [Spec,CP], things are somewhat more complicated.

For certain verbs—*e.g.*, *wonder* and *ask*, it can be assumed that they semantically select Q (à la Grimshaw (1979), except that she has all *wh*-embedding predicates s-selecting Q). However, this doesn't seem quite so straightforward for the many vague predicates for which, as discussed in chapter III, section 5.2, the question of whether they presuppose their complement or not is highly context-sensitive. We cannot simply say that they either s-select Q or do not. We might allow that Q is lexically associated with these predicates, which are not inherently factive (unlike *e.g. know* and *be surprised*), and operates as a default, but may be overridden by contextual factors. I acknowledge problems of implementation here, but it is the best suggestion I have come up with. It is also plausible to assume it is lexically associated with such non-*wh*-clause-embedding predicates as *want (to)* and *persuade (to)*, which participate in interrogative structures (*cf.* chapter III, section 5.4), so that when these combine with an inherently factive *wh*-clause-embedding predicate like *know*, it loses its presuppositionality, as we have seen.

We may conceive of the Q operator semantically in two different ways. One is as a variable-binding, but nonquantifying, operator. As such, it would bind free *wh*-variables in its scope, thus preventing them from getting bound by a quantifier in the higher clause. Alternatively, Q might be viewed, not as a variable-binding operator, but as an opacity-inducing operator, somewhat like the negation operator in certain analyses. In this case, Q would prevent the clause it has scope over from being bound (or quantified) into from a higher clause. For both of these conceptions, the question arises, is it possible for a non-*wh*-phrase, say an indefinite, that (at S-structure) occurs within a nonpresupposed *wh*-clause, to be quantified by a matrix adverb of quantification? The kind of example I have in mind is illustrated by the following sentence:

(138)   The principal seldom wonders which classes a student enrolls in.

The question is, can this mean that few students are such that the principal wonders which classes they enroll in?

Unfortunately, my intuitions are very unclear here. (There are also complications because of the possibility of there being a quantification over enrolling situations. Moreover, if this reading is possible, it raises the theoretically nontrivial question of how the indefinite would get into the restrictive term of the matrix quantifier, given that the matrix predicate is nonpresuppositional.) But let us, for the sake of argument, assume that it is possible. In order to account for it on the variable-binding conception, Q would have to be constrained to bind only *wh*-phrases, and not indefinites; this would mean it is not an unselective binder, in contrast to adverbs of quantification. On the opacity-inducing conception, the opacity would have to hold only for variables that are new within the scope of Q; *i.e.*, if an indefinite, for example, can move (or be copied) out of the Q-headed clause (as would be necessary for it to become part of the restrictive term of the matrix quantifier), then its trace (or copy) could not count as opaque to quantification from the higher adverb. I know of no independent way to decide between these two alternatives, and have no a priori preference, so I will arbitrarily choose one—the opacity-inducing version.[16] (Note that, if the indefinite in (138) cannot be bound by the matrix adverb, then it has no interaction with Q at all, since it can always be bound within its own clause, either within the nuclear scope by existential closure, or within the restrictive term, by a default quantifier (generic or universal) if there is no explicit one.)

For the sake of illustration, I give the LFs for the sentences in (42.a) and (109.a) (in the former, I've thrown in an extra adverb of quantification just to reiterate its lack of effect on the embedded *wh*-phrase):

(139)

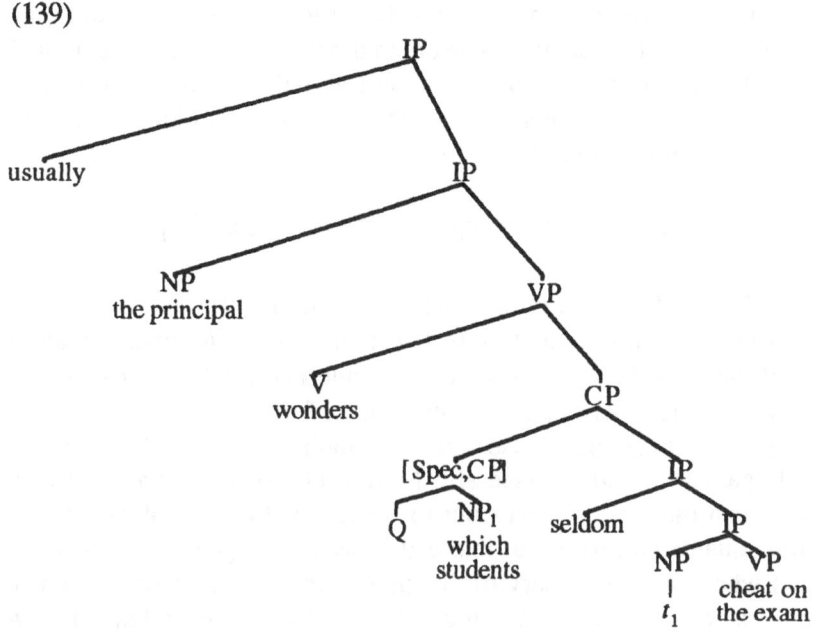

(140)

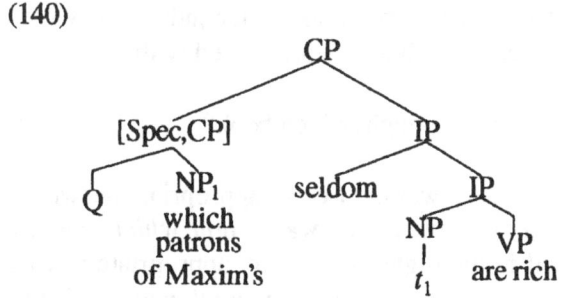

These will translate into the following respective logical formulas:

(141) a. MOST [TIME(t)][wonder$'$(tp,(Q [student$'(x)$ & FEW [TIME(t')][cheat-
on-the-exam$'(x,t')$]),$t)$]

b. Q[patron-of-Maxim's$'(x)$ & FEW[TIME(t)][be-rich$'(x,t)$]]

The result of evaluating Q-headed structures such as these will be sets
of propositions, as in Hamblin's interpretation of questions; the
members of such a set are determined by assigning an appropriate value
to each of the free variables within the structure. (Bear in mind that,
because indefinites can always get bound by an embedded IP-adjoined
quantifier, the only variables that will actually be free within this
structure will be those that translate the *wh*-phrases within the clause.)
This interpretation algorithm is formalized in (142):[17]

(142) $\|Q\varphi\|^{M,g} = \{p: \exists(x_1...x_n)[p = \|\varphi\|^{M,g'}]\}$, where $g' \approx_\varphi g$.

Although my use of the Q-operator is quite different from that of
Baker (1970), I'd like to close this section by showing that, if I adopt
one of the uses Baker proposes for Q, some interesting results follow.
Baker also uses Q as a clausal scope-marker for *wh*-phrases; further, he
proposes that every *wh*-clause, direct and indirect, contains Q. I have argued against the latter[18] (see also Munsat (1986)); however, the idea
that Q can mark scope turns out to interact with my analysis of *wh*-
phrase quantifiability in an interesting way. It appears that the only
cases where it is necessary to distinguish the clausal scope of a *wh*-
phrase is in sentences combining a direct *wh*-question and *in situ wh*-
phrases. This was first pointed out by Baker (1968), who observes that
the sentence in (143) has two interpretations, depending on which
clause the *in situ wh*-phrase, which book, is associated with.

(143) Who remembers where we bought which book?

If this NP is interpreted in the lower clause, an appropriate answer to
(143) would be: *Mary remembers where we bought which book*. If
which book is interpreted in the higher clause, an appropriate answer
would be: *Mary remembers where we bought the math book and John
remembers where we bought the physics book*. In terms of my Q-
operator analysis, on the first reading only *who* is governed by Q,
while on the second reading both *who* and *which book* are governed by
Q (I mean, in the same [Spec,CP] as Q). It seems that, in general, an

in situ wh-phrase may have the scope of any *wh*-phrase in [Spec, CP].[19] Now, it is interesting that this scope ambiguity appears to obtain in the presence of an adverb of quantification; consider the following sentence:

(144) Which professors usually find out which students cheat on which exams?

I believe that the phrase *which exams* in this sentence can be interpreted either in the lower or the higher clause. In the first case, the sentence is asking for the set of professors for each of whom it is true that, for most pairs of a student and an exam the student cheats on, s/he (*i.e.* the professor) finds out that the student cheats on the exam. On the second reading the sentence is asking for the set of pairs of a professor and an exam such that, for most students who cheat on the exam, the professor finds out that the student cheats on the exam. Now, on the assumptions I have been making, *wh-in-situ* is a case of *wh*-movement at LF in English. On one reading, the *in situ* phrase moves to the embedded [Spec,CP], on the other reading, to the matrix [Spec,CP].[20] These two readings correspond, on my analysis, to the respective translations in (145):

(145) a. Q[professor'(x) & MOST[student'(y) & exam'(z) & cheat-on'(y,z)]][find-out'(x,[student'(y) & exam'(z) & cheat-on'(y,z)])]]

       b. Q[professor'(x) & exam'(z) & MOST[student'(y) & cheat-on'(y,z)]][find-out'(x,[student'(y) & exam'(z) & cheat-on'(y,z)])]]

The reader may check that successive application of the evaluation algorithms in (142) and (10) of chapter I to these translations yields the two interpretations for (144) I have paraphrased.

5 Summary

I have shown that there is an asymmetry with respect to the quantifiability of *wh*-phrases and indefinites, notwithstanding the many parallels in their quantificational behavior discussed in chapter III. The asymmetry is that *wh*-phrases are unable to get quantified by a same-clause quantifier. I have argued that this observation follows from that grammatical fact that these phrases, unlike indefinites, undergo syntactic displacement to a position outside the scope of the IP-adjoined quantifier—*wh*-movement. This effect is crucially represented at LF, and moreover, I have argued that it may also occur at LF—always, in languages such as Japanese, and in the case of multiple-*wh*-constructions, also in languages such as English. I have also proposed that the effect of (local) presupposition accommodation be represented at LF —this accounts for the difference in the logical translation between indirect *wh*-questions and free relatives, the former being copied into the restrictive term by accommodation, that latter being moved into the restrictive term. Finally, I have shown that Hamblin's analysis of questions, as sets of propositions that are appropriate alternatives, is straightforwardly importable into mine, and done so by means of an opacity-inducing (or variable-binding) Q-operator, that prevents the *wh*-phrases in its scope from being quantified by any higher quantifier. In addition, this Q-operator displays the kind of scoping properties that Baker noted for *wh*-phrases.

Notes

1. There is yet a third reading, to the effect that rich people in general are such that they often eat at Maxim's, *i.e.*, the adverb has a frequency interpretation, while the indefinite has generic force (*cf.* (109.b)). The latter reading has been analysed analogously to the adverb of quantification case, that is, a quantifier with generic force has been posited; *cf.* Wilkinson (1991), Diesing (1990b) for details and discussion. In this study I will leave the generic reading aside.

2. There is a class of apparent exceptions to this generalization; I return to this in appendix A, where I try to show that they can be accounted for in a way that does not contradict the generalization.

3. The notation [Spec,XP] to refer to the nonprojected node immediately dominated by a maximal projection XP seems to be the recent common practice, though I have not been able to track down its introduction; the notation in Chomsky (1970), where the concept and terminology were introduced, is [Spec,X'], where X' is the sister of the specifier node. The notation [Spec,X] has also appeared in print, for example in Sportiche (1988).

4. While both [Spec,IP] and [Spec,VP] are possible sites of indefinite subjects at LF, it may be in a given sentence that only one option is available; that is, the ambiguity seen in (111), for example, does not always obtain (*cf.* (107.b), where the indefinite only has the force of the adverb, not (just) existential force). This issue has been investigated in detail by Diesing (1990b), drawing on work of Carlson (1977) and Kratzer (1989). Another issue that Diesing examines is the possibility of indefinite objects being in the restrictive term: since they are clearly within the VP in the syntax (unless they have been topicalized or, in certain languages, scrambled), this can only be done by adjunction to IP, within the scope of the quantifier, much in the manner of Heim's general process for deriving LFs.

5. The claim is in fact generally assumed as well in theories that do not employ transformations, *e.g.* LFG (Bresnan, ed. (1982)) or GPSG (Gazdar *et al.* (1985)).

6. In a certain sense, the *which*-phrase in (127) is contextually supplied; this is even clear in the following sentence:

(i)   A farmer usually knows which of these crops bring a good price.

But the meaning of this sentence is: for some contextually supplied set of crops, for most pairs of a farmer and a crop from this set that brings a good price, the farmer knows that the crop brings a good price. The quantificational part of this interpretation is exactly as in (127), thus obtainable from (125) but not from (126). As for the contextually supplied set here, I believe this is due to globabl accommodation of the *which*-phrase (though not of the whole clause); I discuss these matters more in appendix B (see also below in this subsection).

7. Note that it is evidently not the selectional properties of the matrix predicate that prevent the *wh*-phrase from moving to the specifier of the CP immediately dominated by it: the following sentence is fine:

(i)   John is seldom surprised about which crops a farmer usually knows bring a good price.

Here, of course, the *wh*-phrase does have the quantificational force of the matrix adverb.

8. There is in fact a serious issue here concerning motivating this accommodation. Unlike with indirect questions, accommodation of free relatives does not depend on the matrix predicate presupposing its complement: *like*, for example, is probably not a factive predicate, and *want* certainly is not, yet we have *John usually wants what Mary has*. In Berman (1989), I suggested that free relatives may be inherently definite, therefore presuppositional—definites always presuppose their descriptive content (*cf.* Heim (1982)). However, I now believe that definiteness is subject to global, not local, accommodation (I go into this in more detail in appendix B), thus, even if free relatives are inherently definite (and I'm not sure they are), this would not account for why they must be locally accommodated into the restrictive term. Yet, there is no doubt (in my view) that they are so accommodated. At this point I must leave an account of this wanting, but I continue to assume that it does happen.

9. The movement of a category of one type, leaving behind a trace of a different category, has been proposed by Pesetsky (1982) to account for aspects of the distribution of genitive phrases in Russian. It should be noted, however, that what Pesetsky proposes is a change in category (from QP (Quantifier Phrase) to NP), while on the structure

(131) I have assumed for free relatives, both categories are underlyingly present.

10. In fact, it may be possible to assume that presupposition accommodation from the nuclear scope always is movement, instead of copying. In the case of indirect questions, this would leave behind a coindexed CP, which in the logical translation would have to be reconstructed from the CP in the restrictive term in order to get the right interpretation; such reconstruction might be taken to be required by recoverability of deletion (or some such principle). If this is tenable, it would reduce the number of structure-transforming operations in the grammar (assuming resconstruction to be independently required, as seems likely), which is often thought desirable.

11. Nevertheless, it is not necessary on my analysis, given the semantic interpretation rule (10) of chapter I. That operates on the purely logical representations, and in these the effect of presupposition accommodation is certainly (and unproblematically) evident, as I have argued for at length. It should be noted, though, that rejecting (125) does entail one of two restrictions on an LF such as (122): either variable-binding is not represented (*e.g.* by indexing) here, or else existential closure is not represented here. If both were the case, then the *wh*-phrase in the complement clause would be bound within the matrix VP, yielding an existential interpretation, which the *wh*-phrase cannot in fact have. It seems that the easiest thing to do is not to represent the effect of existential closure at LF, but leave it to the semantic interpretation, as I have done in (10) (following Kamp (1981) and the file-change version of Heim (1982)).

12. While the superiority facts are unquestionably syntactic in that they distinguish between differently ordered surface strings, there have been nonsyntactic analyses of them; *e.g.* Bolinger (1978), who proposes to account for acceptable violations of Superiority in terms of the distinction between given and new information, a purely discourse-based distinction.

13. Pesetsky's arguments based on Japanese, which make crucial appeal to LF pied-piping of *wh*-phrases, following Nishigauchi (1986; 1990) and Choe (1987), would not be affected; but these arguments have been contested by Kuno and Masunaga (1987), Fiengo *et al.* (1988), and Kawasaki (1989).

14. Given the phrase structure I have been assuming, and the adjunction of quantifiers to IP in LF, my analysis has to employ the standard notions of scope relations, rather than those defined in May (1985), for example. There, two phrases have the same scope domain, even if one is higher in the tree than the other, as long as both are contained within the same maximal projection, where containment means being dominated by all segments of a node. It is the latter idea that is incompatible with the assumptions of my analysis: a quantifier adjoined to IP is not contained within IP, according to May's theory, since it is not dominated by all segments (occurrences) of the IP; but then it has the same scope domain as the wh-phrases in [Spec,CP], thus no longer excluding the quantifying of the latter by the former, hence not accounting for the quantificational asymmetry.

15. Their motivation for this comes from so-called parenthetical verbs (*cf.* Urmson (1952)); thus it is possible to say *Who, I wonder, left?* but not **Who, I know, left?*. But the class of parenthetical verbs is far smaller than those I would treat as being associated with the Q operator.

16. Nishigauchi (1986; 1990) employs a variable-binding Q-operator, though it differs both syntactically and semantically from the possibility I have discussed, being more like an adverb of quantification; this seems to be problematical, *cf.* Kawasaki (1989). Asher (1987) uses an opacity-inducing Q-operator in order to block anaphoric relations between the matrix clause and the indirect question; he is not concerned with quantifiability, thus the semantics he provides is different from that I give.

17. This definition is essentially the same as that given in the appendix to von Stechow and Zimmermann (1984), except they do not make use of the Q-operator (their analysis is interpretive, not representational as is mine). (In addition, I have not included their provisions making the resulting propositions compatible with and not entailed by the questioner's knowledge—these conditions have to do with the pragmatics of interrogativity.) As von Stechow and Zimmermann note (p.37), an account in these terms "might lead to a revival of Hamblin's theory of questions." This is precisely what I have attempted to do (for nonquantifiable *wh*-phrases), within the general framework of the LHK theory.

It might be thought that, rather than identifying the denotation of a Q-bound structure with the entire set of propositions resulting from assignment of values to the free variable, its denotation should be a subset of this set; after all, sentences such as *Who left?* and *John wonders who left.* are not, in most utterance contexts, understood to be about the leaving of any possible individual. But I have already acknowledged this by stipulating that the values be "appropriate," *i.e.* determined according to the context. Given this, it seems superfluous to reinforce this context-dependeny by a restriction to subsets of the set of possible "answers"; but this seems to be a question of terminological preference.

18. Such a move is also syntactically unnecessary, given the designated landing site for *wh*-movement, [Spec,CP], as well as subcategorization for [+*wh*] CP; Baker's framework lacks these features.

19. Delimiting the distribution and interpretion of *wh-in-situ* is actually quite complicated, though even an adequate superficial discussion of it goes beyond the scope of this dissertation; *cf.* Pesetsky (1987), Comorovski (1989), and references there.

20. There is a problem with this conception of how the second reading is obtained. It constitutes either a violation of Subjacency (Chomsky (1973)) or of the strict cyclicity of movement. It is quite clear that these conditions must be observed at S-structure. But the movement in question (of an *in situ* wh-phrase) occurs in any case only at LF; therefore, one possibility is to stipulate that these conditions, or at least Subjaceny, if strict cyclicity is regarded as inviolable, only apply at S-structure. This is the conclusion (with respect to Subjacency) reached, on entirely independent grounds, by Huang (1982a,b) and Lasnik and Saito (1984) (though contra *e.g.* Nishigauchi (1986; 1990), Choe (1987) and Pesetsky (1987)).

Appendix A

Wh-Phrases as Variables Over Functions

I developed my account in chapter V on the basis of the generalization arrived at in section 2 there, that *wh*-phrases always have wide scope with respect to a same clause quantifier; however, there is a well-known type of case that appears to be a clear counterexample to this position, *i.e.* in which a quantifier appears to have scope over a *wh*-phrase. A direct question serves to illustrate the point:

(146) Which wine did every patron order?

This can mean that there is one kind of wine ordered by all the patrons, *e.g.* Merlot; on this reading the *wh*-phrase has scope over the quantified NP. But there is also a reading according to which each patron ordered a possibly different wine from the other patrons, *e.g.* Smith Merlot, Jones Pinot Grigio, etc: this is the reading where the quantified phrase seems to have scope over the *wh*-phrase. This type of reading was in fact noticed by May (1977) and led May (1985) to propose a different analysis, according to which at LF *wh*-phrases and quantifiers with sentential scope have the same scope domain, therefore sanctioning both readings. But, as I pointed out in chapter V, note 14, this account is incompatible with my analysis of the *wh*-phrase quantificational asymmetry. The question then is, how can I account for the apparent wide scope of the quantified NP in (146)? I think the answer may be found in the treatment of similar cases by Engdahl (1985) and G&S (1984, ch.III).

Engdahl (1980) observed that sentences such as (146) can be answered not only by giving a list of pairs of a patron and a wine he ordered, but also by saying, *e.g.*, *His favorite.* or *The one his best friend recommended.*, etc. Clearly the value of the *wh*-phrase varies with that of the quantified NP in these cases. While this can easily be accommodated by giving the quantified NP wide scope, or equivalently quantifying the NP into the question meaning, Engdahl and G&S have given convincing arguments that such a solution cannot work in general. One is that the same kind of functional relationship between the *wh*-phrase and the quantified NP obtains when the latter is nonuniversal, as in *Which wine did no/many/few patrons order?*, that is, *His favorite.* is still an acceptable answer; yet a list of pairs is not acceptable. Another argument against quantifying in, or giving the quantified NP wide scope at LF comes from a reading when such a *wh*-clause is embedded, as in the following example:

(147) John knows which wine every patron ordered.

John might, for instance, know that every patron ordered his favorite wine without being able to give a list of pairs of a patron and a wine he ordered.

In light of these cases, Engdahl and G&S proposed to take the functional relationship at face value, and, instead of translating the *wh*-phrase with a variable over individuals, translate it with a variable over functions from individuals to individuals, *i.e.* a kind of Skolem function.[1] This allows the denotation of the *wh*-phrase to vary with that of the quantified NP while at the same time not being structurally within its scope. This proposal can be straightforwardly incorporated into my analysis; as an example, I give the logical translation of (146):

(148) ALL[$\forall x$[wine'$(f(x))$]] & ALL[patron'(x)][order'$(x,f(x))$]][know'(j,
       [$\forall x$[wine'$(f(x))$]] & ALL[patron'(x)][order'$(x,f(x))$]])])

In this translation, the universal quantifier $\forall$ closes off the argument of the function-variable, thus allowing the constant wine' to retain the type $\langle e,t \rangle$ of a predicate. An alternative procedure would be to allow the constant to have shifting type; then the argument of the function-variable can be omitted from the logical translation, so that instead of (148), we'd have the following translation:

(149) ALL[wine'(f) & ALL[patron'(x)][ordered'(x,f)]][know'(j,[wine'(f)
       & ALL[patron'(x)][ordered'(x,f)]])])

In this translation, the type of wine' depends on the arity of f; this can be recovered by a default lexical rule, as follows. In general each basic predicate must have a family of translations such that, where $\uparrow P$ represents an appropriately type-raised translation of the basic predicate translation P and f is an n-place function over individuals (or curried function over n individuals), $\uparrow P(f) = \forall x_1..x_n P(f(x_1,...,x_n))$. (Engdahl shows that the function-variable can take multiple arguments, hence the stipulation of n-arity.)[2]

There might seem to be no substantive issue in the choice between (148) and (149); in any case, it is not a crucial matter for present purposes. Still, it may be noted that (149) avoids the introduction into the translation of another quantified structure, which moreover is not a restricted quantification structure (and although it could be represented as one, this would seem to be unenlightening, since it would be something like ALL [INDIVIDUAL(x)] [wine'($f(x)$)]). In addition, (148) forces the representation of selectivity, since otherwise the wider-scope quantifier (ALL, here) would never be able to bind the function-variable; with (149), this contingency does not arise. Furthermore, it must be ensured that the variables which are arguments of the function-variable also occur in the translations of the quantified phrases, although the latter are introduced in the translation separately; whereas, with (149), this is guaranteed by the lexical rule. Finally, it is not unreasonable to hypothesize that, given the necessity of n-place function variables as potential arguments in the first place, general principles of type-shifting, as discussed *e.g.* in Partee (1987) and Hendriks (1990), will automatically yield the needed family of translations for (149), *i.e.* they needn't be separately listed in the grammar. For these reasons I would tend to prefer (149) as the representation of the functional reading, but again, the choice is not of empirical consequence.

In both translations, to return to the issue at hand, I have as usual assumed a default universal quantifier for the *wh*-phrase; in addition I have represented the quantified NP by means of a tripartite restricted quantification structure with the main restrictive term. Most importantly, the function f must be specified: this is already partly done by having f be an argument of the predicate *wine*; in particular, we have that where f is a variable of type $\langle e,e \rangle$, for any individual variable x, $f(x)$ is a wine. But there must be further specification in order to avoid unwanted side effects of quantifying over functions. The restrictions added by the rest of the clause do not suffice, because there are a great many ways of functionally relating a patron and a wine that he ordered that do not conform to the close relationship between patron and wine expressed by a phrase such as 'his favorite wine,' nor indeed are expressible by any simple (*i.e.* nonconjunctive) phrase, for instance, by randomly picking element from the domain and range. The issue here has been noticed by G&S and Engdahl, and they suggest that both contextual factors and some notion of natural, or conventional, functional relationships must be incorporated into the analysis in order to satisfactorily restrict the domain of functions to be quantified over (G&S say (1984, 199) that the functions must be "in some sense computable, or they must be made computable by the context.") This restriction can be represented directly in the logical translation by including a free predicate variable over these Skolem-functions, as G&S do. Alternatively, there might be general felicity conditions on the use and interpretation of function variables, as is implicit in Engdahl's analysis. It bears notice, incidentally, as Engdahl and G&S point out, that the need to restrict the domain is a general problem with quantifying over functions; it arises not only on the functional interpretation of *wh*-phrases, but also on analogous interpretations of indefinites and pronouns.

It is worth pointing out, in this connection, that if the Skolem-functions are not restricted in this way to certain conventional or contextually "computable" kinds, then their specification amounts to giving a list of pairs (or, generally, *n*-tuples). And indeed, this interpretation is available for (146), which might, for example, be continued by saying "namely, Mary ordered Zinfandel, Bill Petite Sirah,...." G&S call this the pair-list reading, and distinguish it semantically from the functional reading, deriving it by quantifying the quantified NP into the *wh*-clause meaning. Such a move is not compatible with my analysis, since it means in effect giving a quantified NP scope over a same-clause *wh*-phrase, which I have argued cannot be the case. It seems to me, however, that G&S's grounds for distinguishing the pair-list and functional interpretations are not conclusive, the strongest one, as I noted above, being the impossibility of a list-of-pairs answer when the quantified NP has less than universal force; but there may well be independent pragmatic or semantic reasons for this, having to do with way items in a list are determined, as G&S themselves suggest. If this is so, there is no need to resort to quantifying in (or scoping the quantified NP over the *wh*-phrase), and the structural relation I have proposed to hold at LF between the two phrase types can be maintained in full generality.

That *wh*-phrases must be translatable as free function variable in my analysis is indicated by sentences such as the following:

(150) John mostly knows which wines every patron ordered.

This sentence would be true on a functional reading in a situation in which, for example, each patron ordered all of the following: his favorite wine, the wine his best friend recommended, and the wine he saw advertised in the paper this morning, but John only knows that every patron ordered his favorite wine and the wine his best friend recommended. This shows that a *wh*-phrase can be functionally dependent on a quantifier within its structural scope while at the same time being itself quantified from a higher adverb of quantification.[3]

The treatment of *wh*-phrases as variables over functions of individuals can be fully assimilated to my analysis of *wh*-phrases as containing a free individual variable by admitting zero-place function variables, *i.e.* of type *e*: these are just individual variables (this is what Engdahl does). But while the zero-place "functional" interpretation—*i.e.* the normal variable interpretation—of *wh*-phrases is quite general, and where it fails to obtain the reasons are also quite general, functional interpretations of higher arity, *i.e.* where the interpretation of the *wh*-phrase depends on that of some other expressions, appear to be rather restricted; in particular, they seem to be triggered only by the presence of a determiner-quantified NP; it does not arise under purely adverbial quantification, as the following sentences illustrate:

(151) a. John always knows which wines which patrons ordered.
 b. John always knows which patrons ordered which wines.

These sentences, in contrast to (147), cannot be continued by saying, *e.g.* "namely, his favorite," which indicates that the functional reading is not available. They can, however, like (147), be continued by giving a list of pairs. This can in fact be taken as support for the generality of the use of function variables, if the pair-list interpretation is rendered by means of them, as I suggested above. In that case it still needs to be explained why the "strict" functional reading is lacking in these sentences. I won't attempt to do this here, but a question perhaps worth

investigating is whether there is a connection between quantificationally closed expressions, such as determiner-quantified NPs, and natural
or conventional functional relations, as appear to be required on the
strict functional reading.[4]

Notes

1. Engdahl (1985, 253(n.10)) maintains that what she calls relational variable are different from variables over Skolem functions, but I fail to see the distinction.

2. Thanks to Ede Zimmermann for helpful discussion of this alternative.

3. I have been told independently by two people that they do not get this reading for (30), at least not saliently. The reading they got was that for most patrons, for every wine they ordered, John knows that they ordered that wine. This has exactly the opposite quantificational relationships as the reading my analysis predicts (and I myself get), and indeed, I see no obvious way of getting such a reading at all within the overall form of my analysis. I have not investigated sentences such as (30) extensively enough to offer any explanation for this discrepancy; but since, at least in the more straightforward examples that I have presented throughout this dissertation, the quantificational variability of wh-phrases in general seems quite robust, and has been corroborated by many people, I will continue to assume that the general form of my analysis is viable, and leave the question of the status of sentences such as (30) open.

4. In this connection it is worth noting that, in addition to determiner-quantified NPs, the strict functional reading is also induced by definite plurals:

(i)   John knows which wines the guests ordered, namely, their favorite.

Definites might also be thought of as quantificationally closed, and indeed have been analysed as a kind of universal quantification (*e.g.* Barwise and Cooper (1981)). (I discuss definites in appendix B, though I do not address this issue.)

Appendix B

Definiteness and Global Accommodation

In my discussion in chapter III of presupposition accommodation I alluded to the distinction made by Heim (1983b) between local and global accommodation (cf. note 17 there); I returned to this in chapter V, section 3.3, where I suggested that the effect of local accommodation may be plausibly represented at LF, but that this seems less plausible for global accommodation. In this appendix I want to consider in more detail the effect of global accommodation on the logical translations (I will make no reference here to LF). In particular, I will try to exploit this process to take into account a widely assumed property of *which*-phrases that I have, for simplicity, purposely ignored throughout this study; namely, that they are definite (this is the position, for example, of Katz and Postal (1964)).

Definites are often said to carry a presupposition of existence; this is the position going back to Frege (1892) and developed into a classical analysis by Strawson (1950; 1952) (contra Russell (1905)). Within the LHK theory this idea, and the consequent distinction between definites and indefinites, has been given the following formulation by Heim (1982, 233): "In definites, the descriptive content of the NP is presupposed, whereas in indefinites it is (merely) asserted." In terms of the context-change semantics that Heim develops, this distinction amounts to the claim that the descriptive content of a definite must be part of the background context prior to the utterance of the definite, in order for its use to be felicitous; conversely, the descriptive content of an indefinite must not be part of the background context prior to the utterance of the indefinite. By building this distinction into a principle regulating the felicity of discourses (the Novelty/Familiarity Condition), Heim is able to treat definites logically the same indefinites, that is, as open sentences. I want to suggest that the behavior of definite *wh*-phrases (*e.g. which*-phrases), as analysed in this study, can be viewed as essentially consistent with this distinction.

First of all, an additional distinction must be made, between singular and plural definites. In all my examples illustrating the quantifiability of *wh*-phrases, where they contain *which*-phrases these are plural. In general, singular *which*-phrase do not appear able display quantificational variability. Compare, for example, the sentence in (105.a) (chapter V), repeated here as (152.a), with the sentence in (152.b):

(152) a.   The maître d' seldom knows which patrons of Maxim's are rich.
       b.   The maître d' seldom knows which patron of Maxim's is rich.

In contrast to (152.a), the sentence in (152.b) means that there are few times such that the maître d' knows of the one patron of Maxim's who is rich that s/he is rich. (The oddness of this sentence comes from the adverb's being forced to quantify over states of the maître d's knowing.) How can we account for this in terms of my analysis? A standard position (along Strawsonian lines) is that a singular definite carries the presupposition that there is exactly one entity (in the domain of discourse) satisfying its descriptive content. Let us also assume that quantifiers carry certain presuppositions (this also accords with the Strawsonian view; *cf.* Strawson (1952, 176); also Hausser (1976)); in particular, an adverb of quantification such as *seldom* presupposes 'more than once' (thus, in its nonfrequency usage, 'more than one,' like *few*). Given this, if the *wh*-clause in (152) is accommodated into the restrictive term, where it would quantified by *seldom*, there would be a clash of presuppositions.

It is worth noting that the same singular/plural distinction with respect to quantifiability obtains with non-*wh* definites; compare the following two sentences:

(153) a.   If the students cheat on the final exam, the principal usually finds out.
       b.   If the student cheats on the final exam, the principal usually finds out.

While (153.a) has a quantificational reading just like (29.a) (chapter III), (153.b) has no such reading, but the singular definite picks a one particular student, and the adverb has a frequency reading. The difference between (29.a), with an indefinite, and (153.a) is that the definite in the latter means that its reference is restricted to some contextually determined set of students[1] (which, moreover, has more than one member —this can be regarded as a presupposition of plurality). The same thing can be said, too, of the plural *which*-phrase in (152.a).

I would like to suggest the descriptive content of definites is accommodated to the context of utterance, *i.e.*, it is globally accommodated, not locally accommodated. Recall that, in the context of a quantified sentence, local accommodation of material in the nuclear scope is to the the restrictive term. In contrast, globally accommodated material remains independent of the restrictive term. What this amounts to in terms of the logical translation is that global accommodation is beyond the scope of the quantifier, so that any free variable within the accommodated material will not get bound by the quantifier. To illustrate this, let us consider what happens in sentences with an embedded *that*-clause. Recall from chapter III my remark (note 17) that presupposition accommodation of the *that*-complement of *regret* is an instance of global accommodation (as are the cases of telescoping (chapter III, note 15)). This is supported by sentences such as the following:

(154) a. The principal usually finds out that students cheat on the final exam.
     b. The maître d' seldom knows that patrons of Maxim's are rich.

The indefinites in these sentences, unlike those in the corresponding *if*-clauses, and unlike the corresponding *wh*-phrases, do not have the quantificational force of the matrix adverbs, but have generic force (coming from an implicit generic quantifier within the embedded clauses. This is straightforwardly accounted for in terms of my analysis if the result of accommodating these clauses, which are presuppositions of the respective nuclear scopes, is not to the restrictive term, as with *if*- and *wh*-clauses, but beyond it—*i.e.*, global accommodation. The resulting logical translations of the sentences in (154) are the following (where G stands for the generic quantifier)[2]:

(155) a. $[G[student'(x)][cheat-on-the-final-exam'(x)]]$ &
$[MOST[TIME(t)][find-out'(tp,[G[student'(x)][cheat-on-the-final-exam'(x)]],t)]]$

b. $[G[patron-of-Maxim's'(x)][rich'(x)]]$ & $[FEW[TIME(t)][know'(tmd,[G[patron-of-Maxim's'(x)][rich'(x)]],t)]]$

Although the indefinites here are in any case bound by the generic quantifier, there is independent evidence that *that*-clauses are globally, not locally, accommodated. Angelika Kratzer observed (p.c.) that the sentence in (156.a) does not have an interpretation corresponding to the sentence in (156.b), where the *that*-clause appears in an *if*-clause, which is analogous to being in the restrictive term of a quantifier; rather the interpretation of (156.a) is the same as that of (156.c), in which the *that*-clause is independent of the *if*-clause:

(156) a.   If Galileo claims that the earth is round, he knows that the earth is round.
b.   If Galileo claims that the earth is round and the earth is round, he knows that the earth is round.
c.   The earth is round and if Galileo claims that the earth is round, he knows that the earth is round.

Let us return now to the case of plural definites. I suggested above that their descriptive content is characterized by a contextually specified set. And I have proposed that this descriptive content is globally accommodated. But in addition, there is still the effect of local accommodation: as usual, the *wh*-clause should be accommodated into the restrictive term. Since the quantity presupposition of plurals is compatible with that of quantifiers such as *usually, mostly, seldom*, etc., this will not be excluded, as it is with singular definites. I will borrow here from the treatment of plurals in Kamp and Reyle (1990) (though they do not bring the effect of presupposition accommodation into their formulation), and add a condition specifying that the variable in the translation of a plural definite (*wh*- or non-*wh*-phrase) belongs to the context set specifying the descriptive content of the phrase. This results in the following translations, for (152.a) and (153.a) respectively (where X is a variable over sets of individuals):

(157) a. [patron-of-Maxim's'(*X*)] & [FEW[*x* ∈ *X* & patron-of-Max-
im's'(*x*) & rich'(*x*)][know'(tmd,[*x* ∈ *X* & patron-of-Max-
im's'(*x*) & rich'(*x*)])]

  b. [student'(*X*)] & [MOST[*x* ∈ *X* & student'(*x*) & cheat-on-
the-final-exam'(*x*)][find-out'(tp,[*x* ∈ *X* & student'(*x*) &
cheat-on-the-final-exam'(*x*)])]

Notes

1. *Cf.* Westerståhl's (1985) use of context sets to distinguish definite determiners from others; in fact, he treats words such as *the* not as logical determiners but as indicators of context sets, which is very much akin to the approach I am taking here.

2. I refrain, for simplicity, from adding the translations of the definites *the exam*, *the principal*, and *the maître d'*; these would all, of course, be globally accommodated, and have their reference restricted to a single individual.

Appendix C

Complement *If*- and *Whether*-Clauses

In chapter III, section 3.1 I remarked that complement *if*-clauses, unlike adjunct *if*-clauses, are apparently unable to serve as restrictive terms of adverbs of quantification. In this respect they are like *whether*-clauses. In this appendix I will try to bring these constructions into the general form of my analysis.

Let us consider variants of the sentences in (28) from chapter III; to restrict attention now to the complement reading, I have omitted the correlative pronouns in (28) and allowed an alternation between *if* and *whether*:

(158) a. The principal usually finds out if/whether students cheat on the final exam.
    b. Sue usually remembers if/whether a birthday present arrives special delivery.
    c. With few exceptions, Mary knows if/whether students submitted abstracts to conferences.
    d. Bill seldom acknowledges if/whether he gets a good idea from a colleague.
    e. John always discovers if/whether a book is stolen from the library.

It is evident from considering the intuitive meanings of these sentences that the *if/whether*-clauses are not functioning as restrictive terms. For example, (158.a) does not mean that for most students who cheat on the final exam the principal finds out of them that (or whether) they cheat on the final exam. Instead, the *if/whether*-clause serves to offer a set of complementary alternatives concerning the possibility of the students cheating on the final exam.

By offering a set of complementary alternatives I mean a choice between a given situation and its negation; for example, in (158.a), the alternatives are, for each student, either that s/he cheated on the final exam or that s/he didn't. This might be expressed with the following logical translation:

(159) student'(x) & [cheat-on-the-final-exam'(x)] ∨ ¬(cheat-on-the-final-exam'(x))]

Now consider what this means with respect to presupposition. The second conjunct in (159) is of the form $P ∨ ¬P$, and this is a tautology. This means that the truth of (159) (under an assignment) depends only on the first conjunct, student'(x). What this suggests is that, when a *whether-* or complement *if*-clause is accommodated as a presupposition of the nuclear scope, it is only the indefinite subject that is semantically significant; in other words, in effect, it is only the indefinite that is presupposed. (There is, however, a problem here; see below.) This would account for the inability of the *if/whether*-clause as a whole to restrict the adverb of quantification. This result accords with the intuitive meanings of the sentences in (158); thus, (158.a), for example, may be paraphrased as: "For most students, if the student cheats on the final exam, the principal finds out that the student cheats on the final exam, and if the student does not cheat on the final exam, the principal finds out that the student does not cheat on the final exam."

In order to represent this meaning within the framework of my analysis, I will take advantage of the following logical equivalence: [($P → Q$) & (¬$P → R$)] ↔ [(P & Q) ∨ (¬P & R)]. The paraphrase just given is of the form on the left-hand side of this equivalence; in terms of the right-hand side, it would be: "For most students, either the student cheats on the final exam and the principal finds out that the student cheats on the final exam, or the student does not cheat on the final exam and the principal finds out that the student does not cheat on the final exam." This more intuitively expresses the offering of alternatives; in addition, with this version we can avoid introducing the material conditional connective into the translation language, which conforms to our use of restricted quantification without this connective, as noted in chapter I. Here, then, is the translation of (158.a):

(160) MOST[student'(x)]
  [([[cheat-on-the-final-exam'(x)] &
    [find-out'(tp,[cheat-on-the-final-exam'(x)])]) ∨
   ([¬(cheat-on-the-final-exam'(x))] &
    [find-out'(tp,[¬(cheat-on-the-final-exam'(x))])])])]

Here I must acknowledge a difficulty for my approach: I see no way of deriving (160) via presupposition accommodation from the nuclear scope. I should note immediately that the difficulty does not lie in the absence of student'(x) from that term; the following translation is logically equivalent to (160):

(161) MOST[student'(x)]
  [(([student'(x) & cheat-on-the-final-exam'(x)] &
   [find-out'(tp,[student'(x) &
    cheat-on-the-final-exam'(x)])]) ∨
   ([student'(x) & ¬(cheat-on-the-final-exam'(x))] &
   [find-out'(tp,[student'(x) &
    ¬(cheat-on-the-final-exam'(x))])])])]

The nuclear scope in this translation has the form $[(P \ \& \ Q) \ \& \ R] \lor [(P \ \& \ \neg Q) \ \& \ S]$, and this is not equivalent to P. The correct restrictive term would be derived by presupposition accommodation if (159) were taken as the nuclear scope, as alluded to above, but this would yield a wrong translation, paraphrased by: "For most students, the principal finds out that they are students."

If there is indeed no way to get (160) (or (161)) via presupposition accommodation from the nuclear scope, I'm not certain what this entails for my general analysis; perhaps the most optimistic conclusion is that the presuppositional properties of *whether-* and complement *if-* clauses are different from those of *wh-* and adjunct *if*-clauses in ways that remain to be elucidated.

Consider the case of a *whether-* or complement *if*-clause embedded under a nonpresuppositional predicate, as in the following example:

(162) The principal usually wonders if/whether students cheat on the
       final exam.

Here the indefinite is not quantified by the adverb, which can only have
a frequency reading. This is as expected, given the fact that the complement is not presupposed. (162) might be paraphrased as: "Most of the
time, the principal stand in the wondering relation to the question: Do
students cheat on the final exam?" The alternatives in this case are
either that students cheat on the final exam or students do not cheat on
the final exam. This in fact follows on Hamblin's semantics for questions, treating the *if/whether*-clause as a *yes/no*-question. Note that
both alternatives are independent quantificational structures, where the
quantifier has generic force, which the indefinite gets. Thus, the set of
propositions which is the denotation of the embedded clause is, (in
rather clumsy paraphrase): {generically many students cheat on the final
exam, generically many students do not cheat on the final exam.}

Bibliography

Note: Entries preceded by an asterisk are either published versions of the preceding entry, which is the unpublished form cited in the text, or newer works referred to in the preface.

List of abbreviations used in the references:

CLS: Proceedings of the annual meeting of the Chicago Linguistics Society. Published by Chicago Linguistics Society, University of Chicago.

GLSA: Graduate Linguistic Student Association, University of Massachusetts, Amherst.

L&P: *Linguistics and Philosophy*. Kluwer, Dordrecht.

LI: *Linguistic Inquiry*. MIT Press, Cambridge MA.

MITWPL: *MIT Working Papers in Linguistics*. Department of Linguistics, Massachusetts Institute of Technology, Cambridge MA.

NELS: Proceedings of the annual meeting of the North Eastern Linguistics Society. Published by GLSA.

NLLT: *Natural Language and Linguistic Theory*. Kluwer, Dordrecht.

UMOP: *University of Massachusetts Occasional Papers in Linguistics*. Published by GLSA.

WCCFL: Proceedings of the annual West Coast Conference on Formal Linguistics. Published by Stanford Linguistics Association, Stanford University.

Altham, J.E.J. and Tennant, Neil W. (1975) "Sortal Quantification." In Keenan, ed., 46-58.

Aoun, Joseph, Hornstein, Norbert and Sportiche, Dominique (1981) "Some Aspects of Wide Scope Quantification." *Journal of Linguistic Research* 1, 69-95.

Åqvist, Lennart (1965) *A New Approach to the Logical Theory of Interrogatives*. Filosofiska Föreningen, Uppsala.

Åqvist, Lennart (1975) *A New Approach to the Logical Theory of Interrogatives*. Gunter Narr, Tübingen. (Republication of Åqvist (1965), with a new preface and additional references.)

Asher, Nicholas (1987) "A Typology for Attitude Verbs and Their Anaphoric Properties." *L&P* 10, 125-197.

Bacon, John (1965) "A Simple Treatment of Complex Terms." *Journal of Philosophy* 62, 328-331.

Baker, Carl L. (1968) *Indirect Questions in English*. Doctoral Dissertation, University of Illinois, Urbana.

Baker, Carl L. (1970) "Notes on the Description of English Questions: The Role of an Abstract Question Morpheme." *Foundations of Language* 6, 197-217.

Barwise, Jon and Cooper, Robin (1981) "Generalized Quantifiers and Natural Language." *L&P* 4, 159-219.

Bäuerle, Rainer (1979) "Questions and Answers." In Bäuerle, Egli, and Stechow, 61-74.

Bäuerle, Rainer, Egli, Urs and von Stechow, Arnim, eds. (1979) *Semantics from Different Points of View*. Springer, Berlin.

Bäuerle, Rainer and Zimmermann, Thomas E. (1987) "Fragesätze." FSN-Bericht-87-20, Forschungsstelle für natürlich-sprachliche Systeme, University of Tübingen.

*Bäuerle, Rainer and Zimmermann, Thomas E. (1991) "Fragesätze." In A. von Stechow and D. Wunderlich, eds. *Semantics. An International Handbook of Contemporary Research*, 333-348. De Gruyter, Berlin.

Belnap, Nuel D., Jr. (1970) "Conditional Assertion and Restricted Quantification." *Noûs* 4, 1-12.

Belnap, Nuel D., Jr. (1982) "Questions and Answers in Montague Grammar." In Peters, Stanley and Esa Saarinen, eds., *Processes, Beliefs, and Questions*, 165-198. Reidel, Dordrecht.

Bennett, Michael (1977) "A Response to Karttunen on Questions." *L&P* 1, 279-300.

Bennett, Michael (1979) *Questions in Montague Grammar*. Published by IULC, Bloomington IN.

Berman, Stephen R. (1987) "Situation-based Semantics for Adverbs of Quantification." In *UMOP* 12, 45-68. Also appears, slightly abbreviated, in *WCCFL* 6, 17-31 (1987).

Berman, Stephen (1989) "An Analysis of Quantificational Variability in Indirect Questions." In the Proceedings of the Student Conference in Linguistics, *MITWPL* 11, 1-15.

Berman, Stephen (1990) "Towards the Semantics of Open Sentences: *Wh*-phrases and Indefinites." In Stokhof, Martin and Torenvliet, Leen, eds., *Proceedings of the Seventh Amsterdam Colloquium*, 53-77. Institute for Language, Logic, and Information, University of Amsterdam.

Boër, Steven E. (1978) "'Who' and 'Whether': Towards a Theory of Indirect Questions Clauses." *L&P* 2, 307-345.

Bolinger, Dwight (1978) "Asking More than One Thing at a Time." In Hiz, ed., 107-150.

Bonet, Eulàlia (1990) "Subjects in Catalan." Unpublished manuscript, MIT, Cambridge MA.

Bresnan, Joan W. (1972) *Theory of Complementation in English Syntax*. Doctoral dissertation, MIT, Cambridge MA.

Bresnan, Joan and Grimshaw, Jane (1978) "The Syntax of Free Relatives in English." *LI* 9, 331-391.

Bresnan, Joan W., ed. (1982) *The Mental Representation of grammatical Relations*. MIT Press, Cambridge MA.

Carlson, Gregory N. (1977) *Reference to Kinds in English*. Doctoral dissertation, University of Massachusetts. Published by GLSA.

Chierchia, Gennaro (1988) "Dynamic Generalized Quantifiers and Donkey Anaphora." In Krifka, Manfred, ed., *Genericity in Natural Language*. Seminar für natürlich-sprachliche Systeme, Universität Tübingen.

Chierchia, Gennaro (1990) "Anaphora and Dynamic Logic." Unpublished manuscript, University of Amsterdam and Cornell University.

*Chierchia, Gennaro (1992) "Anaphora and Dynamic Binding". *L&P* 15, 111-183.

Chierchia, Gennaro, Partee, Barbara H. and Turner, Raymond, eds. (1989) *Properties, Types and Meaning. Volume II: Semantic Issues*. Kluwer, Dordrecht.

Chisolm, Roderick M. (1963) "The Logic of Knowing." *Journal of Philosophy* 60, 773-795. Reprinted in Roth and Galis, 189-219.

Choe, Jae-Woong (1987) "LF Movement and Pied-piping." *LI 18, 348-353*.

Chomsky, Noam (1970) "Remarks on Nominalization." In Jacobs, Roderick A. and Rosenbaum, Peter S., eds., *Readings in English Transformational Grammar*, 184-221. Ginn, Waltham MA.

Chomsky, Noam (1973) "Conditions on Transformations." In Anderson, Stephen R. and Kiparsky, Paul, eds., *A Festschrift for Morris Halle*. Holt, Rinehart and Winston, New York.

Chomsky, Noam (1986) *Barriers*. MIT Press, Cambridge MA.

Comorovski, Ileana (1989) *Discourse and the Syntax of Multiple Constituent Questions*. Doctoral dissertation, Cornell University, Ithaca NY.

Cresswell, Max J. (1973) *Logics and Languages*. Methuen, London.

Cresswell (1985) *Structured Meanings*. MIT Press, Cambridge MA.

Davidson, Donald and Harman, Gilbert, eds., (1972) *Semantics of Natural Language*. Reidel, Dordrecht.

Declerck, Renaat (1988) "Restrictive *when*-Clauses." *L&P 11, 131-168*.

Diesing, Molly (1990a) "Verb-second in Yiddish and the Nature of the Subject Position." *NLLT* 8, 41-79.

Diesing, Molly (1990b) *The Syntactic Roots of Semantic Partition*. Doctoral dissertation, University of Massachusetts, Amherst. Published by GLSA.

*Diesing, Molly (1992) *Indefinites*. MIT Press, Cambridge MA.

Egli, Urs (1973) "Semantische Repräsentation der Frage." *Dialectica* 27, 363-370.

Egli, Urs (1976) "Zur Semantik des Dialogs." Papiere des Sonderforschungsbereich 99, Universität Konstanz.

Elliott, Dale (1971) *The Grammar of Emotive and Exclamatory Sentences in English*. Doctoral dissertation, The Ohio State University. In *Working Papers in Linguistics* 8, viii-110. Computer and Information Science Research Center, The Ohio State University, Columbus.

Engdahl, Elisabet (1980) *The Syntax and Semantics of Questions in Swedish*. Doctoral disseration, University of Massachusetts, Amherst. Published by GLSA.

Engdahl, Elisabet (1985) *Constituent Questions*. Reidel, Dordrecht.

Farkas, Donca and Sugioka, Yoko (1983) "Restrictive If/When Clauses." *L&P* 9, 225-258.

Fiengo, Robert, Huang, C.-T. James, Lasnik, Howard, and Reinhart, Tanya (1988) "The Syntax of Wh-in-Situ." *WCCFL* 7, 81-98.

Fodor, Janet Dean (1978) "Parsing Strategies and Constraints on Transformations." *LI* 9, 427-473.

Frege, Gottlob (1892) "Über Sinn und Bedeutung." *Zeitschrift für Philosophie und philosophische Kritik* 100, 25-50.

Gabbay, Dov M. and Guenthner, Franz, eds., (1989) *Handbook of Philosophical Logic. Volume IV: Topics in the Philosophy of Language.* Reidel, Dordrecht.

Gallin, Daniel (1975) *Intensional and Higher-Order Modal Logic.* North-Holland, Amsterdam.

Gazdar, Gerald (1979) *Pragmatics: Implicature, Presupposition, and Logical Form.* Academic Press, New York.

Gazdar, Gerald, Klein, Ewan, Pullum, Geoffrey, and Sag, Ivan (1985) *Generalized Phrase Structure Grammar.* Harvard University Press, Cambridge MA.

Gerstner, Claudia and Krifka, Manfred (1987) "Genericity." Unpublished manuscript, Universität Tübingen.

Gettier, Edmund L. (1963) "Is Justified True Belief Knowledge?" *Analysis* 23, 121-123. Reprinted in Roth and Galis, 35-38.

*Ginzburg, Jonathan (1992) *Questions, Queries, and Facts: A Semantics and Pragmatics for Interrogatives.* Doctoral dissertation, Stanford University.

*Ginzburg, Jonathan (1993) "Resolving Questions." Unpublished manuscript, Human Communication Research Centre, University of Edinburgh.

Grewendorf, Günther (1983) "What Answers Can Be Given?" In Kiefer, ed., 45-64.

Grice, H. Paul (1975) "Logic and Conversation." In Cole, Peter and Morgan, Jerry L., eds., *Syntax and Semantics*, vol.3, 41-58. Academic Press, New York.

Grimshaw, Jane B. (1977) *English Wh-Constructions and the Theory of Grammar.* Doctoral dissertation, University of Massachusetts. Published by GLSA.

Grimshaw, Jane B. (1979) "Complement Selection and the Lexicon." *LI* 10, 279-326.

Groenendijk, Jeroen and Stokhof, Martin (1982) "Semantic Analysis of Wh-Complements." *L&P* 5 175-233. Reprinted as chapter II of Groenendijk and Stokhof (1984), 77-164.

Groenendijk, Jeroen and Stokhof, Martin (1984) *Studies on the Semantics of Questions and the Pragmatics of Answers.* Doctoral disseration, Universiteit van Amsterdam.

Groenendijk, Jeroen and Stokhof, Martin (1989) "Type-Shifting Rules and the Semantics of Interrogatives." In Chierchia, Partee, and Turner, 21-68.

*Groenendijk, Jeroen and Stokhof, Martin (1990) "Dynamic Montague Grammar." In L. Kálmán and L. Pólos, eds., *Papers from the Second Symposium on Logic and Language*, 3-48. Akadémiai Kiadó, Budapest.

*Groenendijk, Jeroen and Stokhof, Martin (1991) "Dynamic Predicate Logic." *L&P* 14 39-100.

*Groenendijk, Jeroen and Stokhof, Martin (1992) "A Note on Interrogatives and Adverbs of Quantification." ILLC Prepublication Series for Logic, Semantics and Philosophy of Language LP-92-07, University of Amsterdam. Also appears in C. Barker and D. Dowty, eds., Proceedings of *SALT II* (Working Papers in Linguistics No. 40), 99-124, Ohio State University, Columbus.

*Groenendijk, Jeroen and Stokhof, Martin (1993) "Interrogatives and Adverbs of Quantification." In K. Bimbo and A. Mates, eds., *Proceedings of the 4th Symposium on Logic and Language*, Budapest.

Groos, Anneke and van Riemsdijk, Henk (1981) "Matching Effects in Free Relatives: A Parameter of Core Grammar." In A. Belletti, L. Brandi, and L. Rizzi, eds., *Theory of Markedness in Generative Grammar*, 171-216. Scuola Normale Superiore, Pisa.

Hailperin, Theodore (1957) "A Theory of Restricted Quantification." *Journal of Symbolic Logic* 22, 19-35, 113-129.

Hamblin, C.L. (1958) "Questions." *The Australian Journal of Philosophy* 36, 159-168.

Hamblin, C.L. (1973) "Questions in Montague English." *Foundations of Language* 10, 41-53. Reprinted in Partee (1976), 247-259.

Harrah, David (1984) "The Logic of Questions." In Gabbay, Dov M. and Guenthner, Franz, eds., *Handbook of Philosophical Logic. Volume II: Extensions of Classical Logic*, 715-764. Reidel, Dordrecht.

Hausser, Roland R. (1976) "Presuppositions in Montague Grammar." *Theoretical Linguistics* 3, 245-280.

Hausser, Roland R. (1983) "The Syntax and Semantics of English Mood." In Kiefer, ed., 97-158.

Hausser, Roland R. (1984) *Surface Compositional Grammar*. Wilhelm Fink, Munich.

Hausser, Roland and Zaefferer, Dietmar (1979) "Questions and Answers in a Context-dependent Montague Grammar." In F. Guenthner and S.J. Schmidt, eds., *Formal Semantics and Pragmatics for Natural Languages*. Reidel, Dordrecht.

Heim, Irene (1982) *The Semantics of Definite and Indefinite Noun Phrases*. Doctoral dissertation, University of Massachusetts. Published by GLSA.

Heim, Irene (1983a) "File Change Semantics and the Familiarity Theory of Definiteness." In Bäuerle, Rainer, Schwarze, Christoph and von Stechow, Arnim, eds., *Meaning, Use, and Intepretation of Language*, 164-189. Walter de Gruyter, Berlin.

Heim, Irene (1983b) "On the Projection Problem for Presuppositions." *WCCFL* 2, 114-125.

*Heim, Irene (1993) "Interrogative Semantics and Karttunen's Semantics for *Know*." Unpublished manuscript, MIT, Cambridge MA.

Hendriks, Herman (1990) "Flexible Montague Grammar." Unpublished manuscript, University of Amsterdam.

Higginbotham, James and May, Robert (1981) "Questions, Quantifiers and Crossing." *The Linguistic Review* 1, 41-80.

Hintikka, Jaakko (1962) *Knowledge and Belief*. Cornell University Press, Ithaca NY.

Hintikka, Jaakko (1974) "Questions about Questions." In Munitz and Unger, 103-158.

Hintikka, Jaakko (1976) *The Semantics of Questions and the Questions of Semantics*. Acta Philosophica Fennica, Vol.28, No.4. North -Holland, Amsterdam.

Hintikka, Jaakko (1983) "New Foundations for a Theory of Questions and Answers." In Kiefer, ed., 159-190.

Hirschbühler, Paul (1978) *The Semantics and Syntax of Wh- Constructions*. Doctoral dissertation, University of Massachusetts. Published by GLSA.

Hiz, Henry, ed. (1978) *Questions*. Reidel, Dordrecht.

Hiz, Henry, (1978a) "Difficult Questions." In Hiz, ed., 211-226.

Hoepelman (1983) "On Questions." In Kiefer, ed., 191-227.

Hölker, Klaus (1981) *Zur semantischen und pragmatischen Analyse von Interrogativen*. Helmut Buske, Hamburg.

Huang, C.-T. James (1982a) "Move WH in a Language without WH movement." *The Linguistic Review* 1, 369-416.

Huang, C.-T. James (1982b) *Logical Relations in Chinese and the Theory of Grammar*. Doctoral dissertation, MIT, Cambridge MA.

Hull, R.D. (1975) "A Semantics for Superficial and Embedded Questions in Natural Language." In Keenan, ed., 35-45.

Jacobson, Pauline (1988) "The Syntax and Semantics of Free Relatives (in English)." Unpublished manuscript, Brown University, Providence RI.

Jespersen, Otto (1961[1928]) *A Modern English Grammar on Historical Principles*, Vol. III. Allen & Unwin, London.

Kadmon, Nirit (1987) *On Unique and Non-Unique Reference and Asymmetric Quantification*. Doctoral dissertation, University of Massachusetts. Published by GLSA.

Kamp, Hans (1981) "A Theory of Truth and Semantic Representation." In Groenendijk, Jeroen, Janssen, Theo, and Stokhof, Martin, eds., *Formal Methods in the Study of Language*, 277-321. Mathematisch Centrum, Universiteit van Amsterdam. Reprinted in Groenendijk, Janssen, and Stokhof, eds. (1984) *Truth, Interpretation, and Information*, 1-41. Foris, Dordrecht.

Kamp, Hans and Reyle, Uwe (1990) *From Discourse to Logic*. Unpublished book manuscript, Institut für maschinelle Sprachverarbeitung, University of Stuttgart.

*Kamp, Hans and Reyle, Uwe (1993) *From Discourse to Logic*. Kluwer, Dordrecht.

Karttunen, Lauri (1971) "Implicative Verbs." *Language* 47, 340-358.

Karttunen, Lauri (1973) "Presuppositions of Compound Sentences." *LI* 4, 169-193.

Karttunen, Lauri (1974) "Presupposition and Linguistic Context." *Theoretical Linguistics* 1, 181-194.

Karttunen, Lauri (1977) "Syntax and Semantics of Questions." *L&P* 1, 3-44. Reprinted in Hiz, 165-210.

Karttunen, Lauri and Peters, Stanley (1980) "Interrogative Quantifiers." In Rohrer, Christian, ed. *Time, Tense, and Quantifiers*, 181-205. Max Niemeyer, Tübingen.

Kasher, Asa (1973) "Logical Forms in Context: Presuppositions and other Preconditions." *The Monist* 57, 371-395.

Katz, Jerrold J. and Postal, Paul M. (1964) *An Integrated Theory of Linguistic Descriptions*. MIT Press, Cambridge MA.

Kawasaki, Noriko (1989) "On the Semantics of Wh-Questions in Classical Japanese." Unpublished manuscript, University of Massachusetts, Amherst.

Kawasaki, Noriko (1990) "Minimality Condition on Variable Binding." Unpublished manuscript, University of Massachusetts, Amherst.

Keenan, Edward L., ed. (1975) *Formal Semantics of Natural Language*. Cambridge University Press, Cambridge.

Keenan, Edward L. and Hull, Robert D. (1973) "The Logical Presuppositions of Questions and Answers." In Petöfi, János S. and Franck, Dorothea, eds., *Präsuppositionen in Philosophie und Linguistik*, 441-466. Athenäum, Frankfurt.

Kiefer, Ferenc, ed. (1983) *Questions and Answers*. Reidel, Dordrecht.

Kim, Soo Won (1989) "Wh-phrases in Korean and Japanese are QPs." In the Proceedings of the Student Conference in Linguistics, *MITWPL* 11, 119-138.

Kiparsky, Paul and Kiparsky, Carol (1971) "Fact." In Steinberg, Danny D. and Jakobovits, Leon A., eds., *Semantics*, 345-369. Cambridge University Press, Cambridge. Reprinted from M. Bierwisch and K. Heidolph, eds. (1970) *Progess in Linguistics*, 143-173. Mouton, The Hague.

Kitagawa, Yoshihisa (1986) *Subjects in Japanese and English*. Doctoral dissertation, University of Massachusetts. Published by GLSA.

Kratzer, Angelika (1978) *Semantik der Rede*. Scriptor, Königstein.

Kratzer, Angelika (1981) "The Notional Category of Modality." In H. Eikmeyer and H. Rieser, eds., *Words, Worlds, and Contexts— New Approaches in Word Semantics*. Walter de Gruyter, Berlin.

Kratzer, Angelika (1986) "Conditionals." In *CLS* 22/2: Papers from the Parasession on Pragmatics and Grammatical Theory, 1-15.

Kratzer, Angelika (1988) "Comments on P. Jacobson's 'The Syntax and Semantics of Free Relatives in English'." Delivered at the LSA Annual Winter Meeting, New Orleans.

Kratzer, Angelika (1989) "Stage-Level and Individual-Level Predicates." Unpublished manuscript, University of Massachusetts, Amherst.

Kuno, Susumo, and Masunaga, K. (1987) "Questions with WH Phrases in Islands." In *UMOP* 11, 139-166.

Kuroda, S.-Y. (1988) "Whether We Agree or Not: A Comparative Syntax of English and Japanese." *Lingvisticae Investigationes* 12, 1-47.

*Lahiri, Utpal (1991) *Embedded Interrogatives and Predicates That Embed Them.* Doctoral dissertation, MIT.

Lasnik, Howard and Saito, Mamoru (1984) "On the Nature of Proper Government." *LI* 15, 235-289.

Lees, Robert B. (1963[1960]) *The Grammar of English Nominalizations.* IJAL, Vol.26 No.3 Pt.II. Publication 12 of the Indiana University Research Center in Anthropology, Folklore, and Linguistics, Bloomington IN.

Levi, Isaac (1967) *Gambling with Truth.* Knopf, New York.

Levinson, Stephen C. (1983) *Pragmatics.* Cambridge Univerity Press, Cambridge.

Lewis, David (1972) "General Semantics." In Davidson and Harman, 169-218. Reprinted from *Synthese* 22 (1970), 18-67. Also reprinted in Partee (1976), 1-50.

Lewis, David (1975) "Adverbs of Quantification." In Keenan, ed., 3-15.

Lewis, David (1979) "Scorekeeping in a Language Game." In Bäuerle, Egli, and von Stechow, 172-187. Also in *Journal of Philosophical Logic* 8, 339-359.

Lewis, David (1982) "'Whether' Report." In T. Pauli *et al.*, eds., *320311: Philosophical Essays Dedicated to Lennart Åqvist on his Fiftieth Birthday*, 194-206. Uppsala.

Lindström, P. (1966) "First-order Predicate Logic with Generalized Quantifiers." *Theoria* 32, 186-195.

May, Robert (1977) *The Grammar of Quantification.* Doctoral dissertation, MIT, Cambridge MA.

May, Robert (1985) *Logical Form. Its Structure and Derivation.* MIT Press, Cambridge MA.

McCawley, James D. (1979) "Verbs of Bitching." In McCawley, *Adverbs, Vowels, and Other Objects of Wonder*, 135-150. University of Chicago Press, Chicago. Reprinted from D. Hockney et al., eds., *Contemporary Research in Philosophical Logic and Linguistic Semantics*, 313-332. Reidel, Dordrecht.

Milsark, Gary (1974) *Existential Sentences in English.* Doctoral dissertation, MIT, Cambridge MA.

Montague, Richard (1970) "English as a Formal Language." In Visentini, Bruno et al., eds., *Linguaggi nella Società e nella Tecnica*, 189-224. Edizioni di Comunità, Milan. Reprinted in Thomason, ed., 188-221.

Montague, Richard (1973) "The Proper Treatment of Quantification in Ordinary English." In J. Hintikka, J. Moravcsik, and P. Suppes, eds. *Approaches to Natural Language*, 221-242. Reidel, Dordrecht. Reprinted in Thomason, ed., 247-270.

Mostowski, Andrzei (1957) "On a Generalization of Quantifiers." *Fundamenta Mathematicae* 44, 12-36.

Munitz, Milton K. and Unger, Peter K., eds. (1974) *Semantics and Philosophy*. New York University Press, New York.

Munsat, Stanley (1986) "Wh-Complementizers" *L&P* 9, 191- 217.

Nishigauchi, Taisuke (1986) *Quantification in Syntax*. Doctoral dissertation, University of Massachusetts. Published by GLSA.

Nishigauchi, Taisuke (1990) *Quantification in the Theory of Grammar*. Kluwer, Dordrecht.

Partee, Barbara H., ed. (1976) *Montague Grammar*. Academic Press, New York.

Partee, Barbara H. (1984) "Nominal and Temporal Anaphora." *L&P* 7, 243-286.

Partee, Barbara H. (1987) "Noun Phrase Interpretation and Type-Shifting Principles." In Groenendijk, Jeroen, DeJongh, Dick, and Stokhof, Martin, eds. *Studies on Discourse Representation Theory and the Theory of Generalized Quantifiers*, 119-143. Foris, Dordrecht.

Penrose, Roger (1989) *The Emperor's New Mind*. Oxford University Press, Oxford.

Pesetsky, David (1982) *Paths and Categories*. Doctoral dissertation, MIT, Cambridge MA.

Pesetsky, David (1987) "Wh-in-Situ: Movement and Unselective Binding." In Reuland, Eric J. and ter Meulen, Alice G.B., eds. *Representation of (In)definiteness*, 98-129. MIT Press, Cambridge MA.

*Pesetsky, David (1993) "Topic...Comment." *NLLT* 11, 557-558.

Platts, Mark de B. (1979) *Ways of Meaning*. Routledge & Kegan Paul, London.

Portner, Paul (1990) "Quantification, Situations, and Gerunds." Unpublished manuscript, University of Massachusetts, Amherst.

Quirk, Randolph, Greenbaum, Sidney, Leech, Geoffrey, and Svartvik, Jan (1985) *A Comprehensive Grammar of the English Language.* Longman, London.

Radford, Colin (1966) "Knowledge—By Examples." *Analysis 27, 1-11. Reprinted in Roth and Galis, 171-185.*

Rescher, Nicholas (1962) "Plurality-quantification." *Journal of Symbolic Logic* 27, 373-374.

Rooth, Mats (1985) *Association with Focus.* Doctoral dissertation, University of Massachusetts. Published by GLSA.

Ross, John Robert (1967) *Constraints on Variables in Syntax.* Doctoral dissertation, MIT, Cambridge MA.

Roth, Michael D. and Galis, Leon, eds. (1970) *Knowing. Essays in the Analysis of Knowledge.* Random House, New York.

*Rothstein, Susan D. (1992) "Case and NP Licensing." *NLLT* 10, 119-139.

Russell, Bertrand (1905) "On Denoting." *Mind* 14, 479-493.

Russell, Bertrand (1919) *Introduction to Mathematical Philosophy.* Allen & Unwin, London.

*Sandt, Rob A. van der, (1992) "Presupposition Projection as Anaphora Resolution". Journal of Semantics 9, 333-377.

Schubert, Lenhart K. and Pelletier, Francis Jeffrey (1989) "Generically Speaking, or Using Discourse Representation Theory to Interpret Generics." In Chierchia, Partee, and Turner, eds, 193-268.

Schwarzschild, Roger S. (1989) "Adverbs of Quantification as Generalized Quantifiers." In *NELS* 19, 390-404.

Soames, Scott (1982) "How Presuppositions Are Inherited: A Solution to the Projection Problem." *LI* 13, 483-545.

Soames, Scott (1989) "Presupposition." In Gabbay and Guenthner, eds., 553-616.

Sportiche, Dominique (1988) "A Theory of Floating Quantifiers and Its Corollaries for Constituent Structure." *LI* 19, 425-450.

Stalnaker, Robert C. (1972) "Pragmatics." In Davidson and Harman, 380-397.

Stalnaker, Robert C. (1973) "Presuppositions." *Journal of Philosophical Logic* 2, 447-457.

Stalnaker, Robert C. (1974) "Pragmatic Presuppositions." In Munitz and Unger, eds., 197-213.

Stechow, Arnim von (1989) "Focusing and Background Operators." Arbeitspapier Nr. 6, Fachgruppe Sprachwissenschaft, Universität Konstanz.

Stechow, Arnim von and Zimmermann, Thomas Ede (1984) "Term Answers and Contextual Change." *Linguistics* 22, 3-40.

Strawson, P.F. (1950) "On Referring." *Mind* 59, 320-344.

Strawson, P.F. (1952) *Introduction to Logical Theory*. Methuen, London.

Strawson, P.F. (1974) "Positions for Quantifiers." In Munitz and Unger, eds., 63-79.

Stump, Gregory T. (1985) *The Semantic Variability of Absolute Constructions*. Reidel, Dordrecht.

Thomason, Richmond H., ed. (1974) *Formal Philosophy. Selected Papers of Richard Montague*. Yale University Press, New Haven.

Urmson, J.O. (1952) "Parenthetical Verbs." *Mind*, 480-496.

Westerståhl, Dag (1985) "Determiners and Context Sets." In Benthem, Johan van and ter Meulen, Alice, eds. *Generalized Quantifiers in Natural Language*, 45-71. Foris, Dordrecht.

Westerståhl, Dag (1989) "Quantifiers in Formal and Natural Languages." In Gabbay and Guenthner, eds., 1-131.

Wilkinson, Karina (1986) "Generic Indefinite NPs." Unpublished manuscript, University of Massachusetts, Amherst.

Wilkinson, Karina (1991) *Studies in the Semantics of Generic Noun Phrases*. Doctoral dissertation, University of Massachusetts.

Wunderlich, Dieter (1976) *Studien zur Sprechakttheorie*. Suhrkamp, Frankfurt.

Zimmermann, Thomas Ede (1985) "Remarks on Groenendijk and Stokhof's Theory of Indirect Questions." *L&P* 8, 431-448.

Zimmermann, Thomas Ede (1989) "Intensional Logic and Two-sorted Type Theory." *Journal of Symbolic Logic* 54, 65-77.

Index